THE
ORTHODOX LITURGY

THE
ORTHODOX LITURGY

being

THE DIVINE LITURGIES

OF

S. JOHN CHRYSOSTOM

AND

S. BASIL THE GREAT

AND

THE DIVINE OFFICE OF THE PRESANCTIFIED GIFTS

together with

THE ORDERING OF THE HOLY AND
DIVINE LITURGY

THE OFFICE OF PREPARATION FOR THE
HOLY COMMUNION

THE PRAYERS OF THANKSGIVING
AFTER THE HOLY COMMUNION

OXFORD UNIVERSITY PRESS

1982

Oxford University Press, Walton Street, Oxford OX2 6DP

London Glasgow New York Toronto
Delhi Bombay Calcutta Madras Karachi
Kuala Lumpur Singapore Hong Kong Tokyo
Nairobi Dar es Salaam Cape Town
Melbourne Auckland

and associates in

Beirut Berlin Ibadan Mexico City Nicosia

Published in the United States by
Oxford University Press, New York

ISBN 0 19 143495 7

Printed in Great Britain
at the University Press, Oxford
by Eric Buckley
Printer to the University

PREFACE

THE EASTERN ORTHODOX CHURCH reserves the word *liturgy*, which in the West applies to all Divine Service, for the celebration of the Eucharist. Three forms are used: the Liturgies of S. John Chrysostom and S. Basil the Great (near contemporaries who lived in the fourth century) and the Divine Office of the Presanctified Gifts.

The Liturgy of S. John Chrysostom is the customary liturgy but ten times during the year—on Christmas Eve and the Eve of the Epiphany, on the first five Sundays in Lent, on Thursday and Saturday of Holy Week, and on his feast-day, 1 January—the Orthodox Church celebrates the Liturgy of S. Basil the Great.

The Liturgies of S. John Chrysostom and S. Basil the Great are divided into three parts. In the first part, the *Ordering*, the priest prepares the bread and the wine. The following *Liturgy of the Catechumens* consists mainly of the singing of psalms and the reading of an Epistle and a Gospel lesson, to which during the first centuries of Christianity catechumens (those not yet baptized into the Church) were admitted. The third part, called the *Liturgy of the Faithful*, is the celebration of the sacrament of the Holy Eucharist, at which the early Church permitted only the Faithful—that is, baptized and confirmed members of the Church—to be present.

The Liturgies of S. John Chrysostom and S. Basil the Great differ only in certain of the 'Secret Prayers' (thus termed because pronounced by the officiating clergy in a low voice more generally inaudible to the congregation), one *troparion*, and three phrases in the consecration of the holy gifts.

The Liturgy of the Presanctified Gifts, celebrated only on certain weekdays in Lent, is so called because communion is given from the holy gifts consecrated on the previous Sunday. The Fathers of the Church regarded it as unbefitting the contrition of Lent that the full Liturgy of S. John Chrysostom or S. Basil the Great be celebrated every day during the Great Fast. The Office, which begins with Vespers, is similar in structure to the other two liturgies, except that lessons are read from *Genesis* and the *Proverbs* in place of, or as well as, readings from the Epistle and Gospel; and after the Great Entrance—in which the previously consecrated gifts are brought from the *prothesis* to the altar—everything is omitted until the prayer before the Lord's Prayer. This Office was instituted in the early days of Christianity but is ascribed in its present form to S. Gregory Dialogos, Bishop of Rome in the sixth century.

All creation came symbolically through the mouth: 'In the beginning was the Word . . . and the Word was God.' In constructing their liturgies the Early Fathers sought to formulate their prayers and exhortations in the words of the Scriptures.

The present translations have been made* from the Old Church Slavonic service-books (in consultation with the corresponding Greek texts). Save for a few instances where the original requires the Septuagint Version of the Old Testament, they look to the language of the Authorized King James Version of the Bible or the almost contemporary *Book of Common Prayer*—liturgical English at its noblest. Spelling, punctuation and the use of capital letters likewise conform. Of 'an innumerable multitude' of possible references those suggested in the footnotes are either direct quotations or they give the source of a word or phrase having the same weight and gravity, and offering comparable associations.

The pre-Reformation *Prymers* have similarly proved a fount of inspiration in the work of adaptation from, and into, the genius of the two languages, Old Church Slavonic and liturgical English.

The Liturgy is a Divine Act. 'The Word was made flesh, and dwelt among us . . . full of grace and truth.'

'Heaven and earth shall pass away: but my words shall not pass away.'

---

* Primarily for use by the Stavropegic Monastery of St. John the Baptist at Tolleshunt Knights in Essex.

CONTENTS

THE OFFICE OF
PREPARATION
FOR THE
HOLY COMMUNION

If a priest be present he shall say

Blessed is our God always, now, and for ever:[1] world without end.[2] Amen.

In other wise a layman shall begin

In the name of the Father, and of the Son, and of the Holy Ghost. Amen.

Glory be to thee, O our God, glory be to thee.

O heavenly King and Comforter, Spirit of truth,[3] which art in all places and fillest all things; Treasure of goodness and Giver of life: Come and abide in us, and cleanse us from all that defileth. And save our souls, O thou who art good.

O holy God, Holy and Strong, Holy and Immortal, have mercy upon us.   [*thrice*]

Glory be to the Father, and to the Son, and to the Holy Ghost; now, and for ever: world without end. Amen.

Most Holy Trinity, have mercy upon us. O Lord, purge away our sins.[4] O Master, pardon our transgressions. O Holy One, visit and heal our infirmities, for thy name's sake.[4]

Lord, have mercy.   [*thrice*]

Glory be to the Father, and to the Son, and to the Holy Ghost; now, and for ever: world without end. Amen.

Our Father which art in heaven,[5] Hallowed be thy Name, Thy kingdom come, Thy will be done, in earth as it is in heaven. Give us

---

[1] Isa. 26: 4.   [2] Isa. 45: 17; Eph. 3: 21.   [3] John 14: vv. 16–17.   [4] Ps. 79: 9.   [5] Matt. 6: vv. 9–13; Luke 11: vv. 2–4; *Book of Common Prayer*.

this day our daily bread; And forgive us our trespasses, As we forgive them that trespass against us; And lead us not into temptation, But deliver us from evil.

Priest

For thine is the kingdom, the power, and the glory,[1] of the Father, and of the Son, and of the Holy Ghost; now, and for ever: world without end. Amen.

Lord, have mercy.   [*12 times*]

Glory be to the Father, and to the Son, and to the Holy Ghost; now, and for ever: world without end. Amen.

O come, let us worship God our King. O come, let us worship and bow down[2] before Christ our King and our God. O come, let us worship and bow down before the Very Christ, our King and our God.

And Psalm 23

The Lord is my shepherd; I shall not want.

He maketh me to lie down in green pastures: he leadeth me beside the still waters.

He restoreth my soul: he leadeth me in the paths of righteousness for his name's sake.

Yea, though I walk through the valley of the shadow of death, I will fear no evil: for thou art with me; thy rod and thy staff they comfort me.

Thou preparest a table before me in the presence of mine enemies: thou anointest my head with oil; my cup runneth over.

Surely goodness and mercy shall follow me all the days of my life: and I will dwell in the house of the Lord for ever.

And Psalm 24

The earth is the Lord's, and the fulness thereof; the world, and they that dwell therein.

For he hath founded it upon the seas, and established it upon the floods.

---

[1] 1 Tim. 1: 17.   [2] Ps. 95: 6.

Who shall ascend into the hill of the Lord? or who shall stand in his holy place?

He that hath clean hands, and a pure heart; who hath not lifted up his soul unto vanity, nor sworn deceitfully.

He shall receive the blessing from the Lord, and righteousness from the God of his salvation.

This is the generation of them that seek him, that seek thy face, O Jacob.

Lift up your heads, O ye gates; and be ye lift up, ye everlasting doors; and the King of glory shall come in.

Who is this King of glory? The Lord strong and mighty, the Lord mighty in battle.

Lift up your heads, O ye gates; even lift them up, ye everlasting doors; and the King of glory shall come in.

Who is this King of glory? The Lord of hosts, he is the King of glory.

And **Psalm 116** (vv. 10-19)

I believed, therefore have I spoken: I was greatly afflicted:

I said in my haste, All men are liars.

What shall I render unto the Lord for all his benefits toward me?

I will take the cup of salvation, and call upon the name of the Lord.

I will pay my vows unto the Lord now in the presence of all his people.

Precious in the sight of the Lord is the death of his saints.

O Lord, truly I am thy servant; I am thy servant, and the son of thine handmaid: thou hast loosed my bonds.

I will offer to thee the sacrifice of thanksgiving, and will call upon the name of the Lord.

I will pay my vows unto the Lord now in the presence of all his people,

In the courts of the Lord's house, in the midst of thee, O Jerusalem.

And then

Glory be to the Father, and to the Son, and to the Holy Ghost; now, and for ever: world without end. Amen.

Alleluia. Alleluia. Alleluia. Glory be to thee, O God. [thrice]

Lord, have mercy. [thrice]

And the troparia

O Lord, born of the Virgin,[1]
Regard not my transgressions.
Cleanse thou my heart,
And make of it a temple
For thy most pure body and blood.
Neither cast me from thy presence,
O thou whose mercy cannot be measured.[2]

Glory be to the Father, and to the Son, and to the Holy Ghost.

How dare I to partake of thy hallowed things?[3]
Unworthy as I am?
For if I make bold to draw nigh
Among them that are worthy,
And have not on a wedding garment,[4]
I do but procure the condemnation
Of my most sinful self.
Cleanse my defiled soul, O Lord, and save me,
For thou art loving-kind.

Now, and for ever: world without end. Amen.

Great is the multitude of my transgressions,
O Mother of God,
I turn to thee, thou who art pure,
Seeking salvation.
Visit my ailing soul,
And pray thy Son, our God,
To grant me remission of my evil deeds,
Thou who alone art blessed.

Troparion *for Thursday in Holy Week*

That night after Jesus had washed their feet
The glorious disciples were illumined.[5]
But darkness blinded the eyes[6] of Judas the traitor;[7]
Ailing with covetousness; and unto unjust judges
He betrayed thee, the righteous judge.[8]

---

[1] Luke 1: 27.   [2] Hos. 1: 10.   [3] Num. 5: 10.   [4] Matt. 22: 11.   [5] John 13: vv. 4–20.
[6] 1 John 2: 11.   [7] Luke 6: 16.   [8] Ps. 7: 11 (marginal reading).

O Man who seekest thine own,[1] consider him
Who for possessions' sake went and hanged himself.[2]
Shun him that was greedy of gain;[3]
Who dared such deeds against the Master.

Thou who art gracious unto all, O Lord,
Glory be unto thee.

Lord, have mercy.   [*40 times*]

Then these verses following

O man who desirest to eat of the body of the Lord,
Draw near in fear, lest thou be consumed.
For fire it is.
And drinking the blood of God unto communion,
First be thou reconciled to them that have afflicted thee,
And then with boldness eat of the sacramental food.

Before partaking of the dread sacrifice
Of the life-giving body of the Lord,
After this manner, and in fear and trembling, pray:

1. *A Prayer of S. Basil the Great*

O LORD and MASTER, JESUS CHRIST our GOD, well-spring of life and immortality, Maker of all things visible and invisible, Son co-eternal with the Father; Who in the latter days of thy great goodness wast clothed in flesh, and wast crucified and buried for us thankless and wicked men, and hast by thy blood renewed our nature, corrupted by sin: Do thou, O King immortal,[4] accept the repentance of a transgressor. Incline thine ear unto me, and hear my cry. For I have sinned, O Lord, I have sinned against heaven, and before thee,[5] and am no more worthy to behold the height of thy glory. I have angered thy goodness: I have transgressed thy commandments, and disobeyed thine ordinances. But thou, O Lord, inasmuch as thou art kind,[6] slow to anger, and plenteous in mercy,[7] hast not suffered me to perish with my unlawful deeds;[8] looking at all times for my conversion. For thou who lovest mankind hast said, by the mouth of

---

[1] 1 Cor. 10: 24.   [2] Matt. 27: 5.   [3] Prov. 1: 19.   [4] 1 Tim. 1: 17.   [5] Luke 15: 18.
[6] Luke 6: 35.   [7] Ps. 103: 8.   [8] 2 Pet. 2: 8.

thy prophet: I have no pleasure in the death of the wicked; but that the wicked turn from his way and live.[1] Thou dost not wish, O Master, that the work of thy hands should perish, neither desirest thou the destruction of man; But wilt have all men to be saved, and to come unto the knowledge of the truth.[2] Wherefore even I, unworthy though I be of heaven and of earth and of this transitory life, in that I have made me subject to sin and a lover of pleasures,[3] and have defiled thine image: Yet, inasmuch as I am thy creature and the work of thy hands, I despair not of my salvation, O wretched man that I am![4] And emboldened by thy measureless compassion, I draw nigh. Wherefore accept me also, O Lord and lover of mankind, as thou didst accept the harlot, the thief, the publican, and the prodigal son; And take away the heavy burden of my sins, O thou who takest away the sin of the world,[5] and healest the diseases[6] of mankind, calling unto thee all that labour and are heavy laden and giving them rest:[7] Who camest not to call the righteous, but sinners to repentance.[8] Cleanse me from all filthiness of the flesh and spirit, and teach me to perfect holiness in thy fear:[9] That having the answer of a good conscience,[10] and receiving a portion of thy holy things,[11] I may be joined[12] unto thy sacred body and blood; and may have thee to abide and dwell in me, with the Father and thy Holy Spirit. Yea, O Lord Jesus Christ my God, vouchsafe that I may partake without condemnation of thy most pure and life-giving mysteries; Neither let my soul and body become weak because I have partaken thereof unworthily. But grant me even unto my last breath to partake uncondemned of thy hallowed gifts, unto communion of the Holy Ghost,[13] unto provision for life eternal, and an acceptable defence at thy dread judgment-seat. That I also, together with all thine elect, may be a partaker of thine incorruptible blessings which thou hast prepared for them that love thee, O Lord: in whom thou art glorified for ever. Amen.

---

[1] Ezek. 33: 11.   [2] 1 Tim. 2: 4.   [3] 2 Tim. 3: 4.   [4] Rom. 7: 24.   [5] John 1: 29.
[6] Ps. 103: 3.   [7] Matt. 11: 28.   [8] Matt. 9: 13; Mark 2: 17; Luke 5: 32.   [9] 2 Cor. 7: 1.
[10] 1 Pet. 3: 21.   [11] Ezek. 22: 26.   [12] 1 Cor. 6: 17.   [13] 2 Cor. 13: 14.

2. *A Prayer of S. John Chrysostom*

O LORD my GOD, I know that I am not worthy, neither is it meet, that thou shouldest come under the roof[1] of the temple of my soul. All is desolate therein, and downfallen, and in me thou hast not where to lay thy head.[2] Yet inasmuch as for our sakes thou didst humble thyself from on high, so now do thou descend to the measure of my lowliness; And as thou tookest upon thee to be laid in the manger[3] of dumb creatures, so also graciously vouchsafe to lie in the manger of my empty soul, and enter my defiled body. And as thou didst not disdain to sit at meat with sinners in the house of Simon the leper,[4] so also consent to enter into the humble dwelling of my soul, leprous and sinful though it be. And as thou didst not reject the woman which was a sinner like unto me, when she came to thee and touched thee,[5] so have compassion upon me, a sinner, who now come unto thee and touch thee. May that fiery coal, thy most pure body and thy precious blood, be to me unto the hallowing, enlightning and health of my humble soul and body; unto the relieving of the burden of my manifold sins; unto preservation from the working of Satan;[6] unto the averting and prevention of my evil and wicked ways;[7] unto the mortification of my passions; unto the keeping of thy commandments; unto the increase of thy divine grace; unto an inheritance in thy kingdom.[8] For I do not presume to come unto thee, O Christ-God, except that I am made bold by thine ineffable goodness, and fear lest long absenting myself from communion with thee the ghostly wolf devour me. Wherefore I pray thee, O Master, who alone art holy: Sanctify my soul and body, my mind and my heart. Renew me wholly. Implant thy fear in my members. And let thy hallowing remain with me alway. Be thou my help and my defence. Sustain my life in peace. Deem me worthy to stand at thy right hand among thy saints: Through the prayers and supplications of thy most pure Mother; of the bodiless servitors and heavenly hosts; and of all the saints which have been well-pleasing in thy sight since the world began. Amen.

---

[1] Matt. 8: 8.   [2] Matt. 8: 20; Luke 9: 58.   [3] Luke 2: 7.   [4] Matt. 26: 6; Mark 14: 3.
[5] Luke 7: vv. 37–48.   [6] 2 Thess. 2: 9.   [7] Ezek. 20: 44.   [8] Eph. 5: 5.

3. *A Prayer of S. Simeon Metaphrastes*

O LORD the only pure and incorruptible, who in the ineffable mercy of thy love toward mankind didst assume our nature, being incarnate by the Holy Ghost of the Virgin Mary,[1] by the good will of the eternal Father; O JESUS CHRIST, Divine Wisdom, Peace and Power,[2] who didst take upon thyself the life-giving and redeeming passion of the cross, the nails, the spear, death itself: Do thou destroy the bodily passions that slay my soul. O THOU who by thy burial didst conquer the infernal regions, so do thou overcome my wicked thoughts with good counsel, and blot out the evil spirit. O THOU who by thy life-giving resurrection on the third day didst restore our fallen forefather Adam, do thou restore me who am laid low by sin, putting forth to me the manner of repentance. O THOU whose glorious ascension made human flesh divine, and honoured it by thy sitting on the right hand of the Father, enable me through the partaking of thy sacred mysteries to stand aright among them that are saved. O THOU who by the descent of the Comforter madest the disciples worthy vessels of thy Spirit, so make me likewise to be a receptacle of the same Spirit. O THOU who wouldest come again to judge both the quick and the dead in righteousness, vouchsafe even unto me to behold thee in the clouds, my Judge and my Creator, with all thy saints: That I may ever glorify and praise thee, together with thine eternal Father and thy most holy, good and life-giving Spirit; now, and for ever: world without end. Amen.

4. *Another Prayer of S. Simeon Metaphrastes*[3]

Like as I were now standing before thy dread judgment-seat, O CHRIST GOD, in expectation of sentence, and giving account of the sins that I have committed: So also at this moment, ere the day of condemnation be come, I stand before thee, in the presence of thy holy angels, bent under the weight of my conscience; and confess my evil deeds.

Thou seest, O Lord, my humiliation. Forgive me all my sins. Thou seest how mine iniquities are more than the hairs of mine head.[4] There is no sin, no evil, that I have not committed; that I have not imagined in my heart. I have filled my soul with uncleanness. I have defiled my senses, and am become altogether unworthy.

---

[1] *B.C.P.* Nicæan Creed.   [2] 1 Cor. 1: 24.   [3] [Adaptation.]   [4] Ps. 40: 12.

Wherefore, O King most marvellous, O good and gentle Lord, shew the breadth, and length, and depth, and height[1] of thy mercy even unto me, for there is no sin that can overcome thy loving-kindness.

Accept me, a sinner, as thou didst accept the prodigal son, the thief that was crucified with thee, the woman which was a sinner.[2] Accept me that beyond measure, in the day and in the night, voluntarily and involuntarily, in word and deed and thought, have sinned against thee. And as thou didst receive them that came about the eleventh hour, and bore not the burden and heat of the day,[3] so receive me also. For I have sinned greatly, I have vexed thy holy Spirit,[4] and grieved thy love. Nevertheless, O Lord, render not to me my desert.[5] Rebuke me not in thy wrath: neither chasten me in thy hot displeasure.[6] Have mercy upon me, O Lord, for though I be weak yet am I the work of thine hands.[7] Against thee, thee only, have I sinned;[8] but I pray thee, enter not into judgment with thy servant.[9] If thou, Lord, shouldest mark iniquities, O Lord, who shall stand?[10] I am a bottomless pit of sin, and am not worthy to lift up so much as mine eyes unto heaven,[11] by reason of my sins. I am a reproach of thee, and despised of the people.[12] Who shall raise me from the multitude of my sins? O Lord my God, in thee do I put my trust. If so be I may have hope of salvation; if thy clemency may prevail against my transgressions that are without number, then be thou my Saviour; and according to thy great mercy, remit and forgive all my sins. For my soul hath wrought many evils; and there is no hope of salvation in me. Have mercy upon me, according to thy loving-kindness:[13] and judge me not according to my deeds.

Turn me unto thee. Protect and deliver my soul from mine iniquities that do wax ever worse, and from my wicked imaginations.[14]

Save me for thy mercy's sake, that where sin has multiplied, there also thy grace may abound.[15] And I will praise and laud[16] thee all the days of my life.

For thou art the God of them that repent; and the Saviour of sinners.

---

[1] Eph. 3: 18.   [2] Luke 7: 37.   [3] Matt. 20: vv. 8–12.   [4] Isa. 63: 10.   [5] Ps. 28: 4.
[6] Ps. 38: 1.   [7] Job. 10: 3.   [8] Ps. 51: 4.   [9] Ps. 143: 2.   [10] Ps. 130: 3.   [11] Luke 18: 13.
[12] Ps. 22: 6.   [13] Ps. 51: 1.   [14] Prov. 6: 18.   [15] Rom. 5: 20.   [16] Rom. 15: 11.

And unto thee we ascribe glory, with thine eternal Father, and thy most holy, good and life-giving Spirit; now, and for ever: world without end. Amen.

5. *A Prayer of S. John Damascene*

O LORD and MASTER, JESUS CHRIST our GOD, who alone hast power to absolve the sins of man: For that thou art good and loving-kind, forgive me all my transgressions, witting and unwitting; and vouchsafe that I may partake without condemnation of thy divine and glorious, most pure and life-giving mysteries, neither unto affliction, nor torment, nor the increase of my sins, but unto cleansing and hallowing, and the earnest[1] of the Kingdom and the life to come; unto help and defence, refutation of adversaries, and the purging of my manifold transgressions. For thou art the God of mercy, of bounties and of love toward mankind; And unto thee we ascribe glory, together with the Father, and the Holy Spirit; now, and for ever: world without end. Amen.

6. *A Prayer of S. Basil the Great*

I know, O LORD, that I partake unworthily of thy most pure body and thy precious blood; that I am guilty, not discerning thy body and thy blood, O Christ my God, and do eat and drink damnation to myself:[2] Yet, trusting in thy bounties, I come unto thee, that didst say, He that eateth my flesh, and drinketh my blood, dwelleth in me, and I in him.[3] Wherefore have pity, O Lord, and put me not to rebuke, but deal with me, a sinner, according to thy mercy; And let these holy things be for me unto healing, cleansing and enlightenment, preservation and salvation, and unto the hallowing of soul and body; unto the driving out of every idle thought, and of the works and deceits wrought by the devil within me; unto boldness and love toward thee; unto the reformation of my life, and steadfastness; unto the increase of virtue and perfection; unto the fulfilling of thy commandments; unto fellowship with the Holy Spirit, provisioning for the journey to eternal life, and an acceptable answer at thy dread judgment-seat; not unto judgment nor unto condemnation.

---

[1] 2 Cor. 1: 22; Eph. 1: 14.   [2] 1 Cor. 11: vv. 27, 29.   [3] John 6: 56.

7. *A Prayer of S. Simeon the New Theologian*

From lips defiled, from a vile heart, an unclean tongue and a soul polluted, receive this prayer, O CHRIST; and despise not my words, neither my manner nor mine importunity. Suffer me to speak boldly that which I desire, O my Christ. Nay, teach me rather that which it becometh me to do and to speak. I have sinned more than the woman in the city who, when she knew where thou didst sit at meat, bought ointment and ventured to anoint thy feet,[1] O Christ, my Master[2] and my God. Inasmuch as thou didst not reject her whose heart led her to thee, neither despise thou me, O Word, but suffer me also to clasp and embrace thy feet, and dare to anoint them with a flood of tears, as with a precious ointment. Wash and purify me with my tears, O Word. Forgive me my trespasses, and grant me pardon. Thou knowest the multitude of mine evil-doing. Thou knowest also my wounds, and dost behold my sores.[3] But thou knowest too my faith; thou seest mine intent; thou hearest my sighs. No tear is hidden from thee, O God, my Maker, my Deliverer.[4] Thine eyes behold that which I have not yet done: for in thy book is written that which has not yet come to pass. Consider my lowliness. Look upon mine affliction and my pain.[5] Forgive my every sin, O God of all, that with a pure heart and fearful mind, and with a contrite soul, I may partake of thine undefiled and most holy mysteries, wherewith every man who eateth and drinketh thereof with a pure heart is quickened with life divine. For thou, O Master, didst say, He that eateth my flesh, and drinketh my blood, dwelleth in me, and I in him.[6] True in all ways is the word of my Lord and God. Partaking of the divine grace whereby man becometh like unto God, I am no longer alone but am with thee, O my Christ, light of the world.[7] Suffer me not to dwell apart from thee, O Giver of life, who art my breath, my life, my joy, the salvation of the world. Wherefore I draw nigh unto thee, as thou seest, with tears and a contrite soul: I beseech thee, deliver me from my sins, and grant me to partake without condemnation of thy life-giving and pure mysteries, that according to thy word thou mayest abide in me, of all men the most miserable:[8] lest if I be found without thy grace the tempter should craftily beguile me, and having tempted entice me

---

[1] Luke 7: vv. 37–8.   [2] Matt. 23: 8.   [3] Isa. 1: 6.   [4] Ps. 95: 6; Ps. 70: 5; Rom. 11: 26.
[5] Ps. 25: 18.   [6] John 6: 56.   [7] John 8: 12.   [8] 1 Cor. 15: 19.

from thy precepts which make man god-like. For this cause I fall down before thee, and earnestly cry unto thee: As thou didst accept the prodigal son, and the woman in the city[1] when she came to thee, so also receive me, who am prodigal and vile, O thou who art bountiful. Turning to thee now with a contrite soul, I know, O Saviour, that no man hath so sinned against thee as I, nor done the things that I have done. Yet this also I know, that neither the magnitude of the transgression, nor the multitude of the sins surpasseth the long-suffering patience of my God, and his exceeding love toward mankind. According to thy merciful compassion thou dost cleanse and lighten them that earnestly repent, and makest them to partake of the light, and abundantly to share thy divinity. And strange though it be to angels and to the mind of man, thou dost oft-times hold converse with them as with thy true friends. All which doth render me bold, doth inspire me, O my Christ. And confident of thy rich mercy toward us, both rejoicing and trembling, I who am as grass[2] do partake of fire. And lo, a mighty wonder, I am refreshed and not consumed, even as of old the burning bush was not consumed.[3] Now with thankful mind, with grateful heart, with thankfulness in my soul and body, I worship thee, my God. I glorify thee and I magnify thee, for blessed art thou, now, and for evermore.

8. *A Prayer of S. John Chrysostom*

O GOD, loose, remit, forgive me my transgressions whereby I have sinned against thee, whether in word, or deed, or thought, willing or unwilling, witting or unwitting. Forgive me all, for thou art good and dost love mankind. And by the prayers of thy most pure Mother, of the holy powers that serve thee, and of all the saints which have been well-pleasing in thy sight since the world began, vouchsafe that uncondemned I may receive thy most pure body and thy precious blood, unto the healing of my soul and body, and the purging of my evil imagination.[4] For thine is the kingdom, the power and the glory, together with the Father and the Holy Spirit; now, and for ever: world without end. Amen.

---

[1] Luke 7: vv. 37-8.   [2] 1 Pet. 1: 24.   [3] Exod. 3: 2.   [4] Gen. 8: 21.

9. *Another Prayer of S. John Chrysostom*

I am not worthy, LORD and MASTER, that thou shouldest come under the roof[1] of my soul; But for that thou desirest, O lover of mankind, to dwell in me, I make bold to draw near. Thou biddest me to open the doors that thou, my Creator, mayest enter in with mercy proper to thee, and bring light to my darkened mind. I believe that thou wilt so do. For thou didst not turn from the woman, which was a sinner,[2] when she came to thee with tears. Neither didst thou reject the publican that repented;[3] nor the malefactor when he confessed thy kingdom.[4] Nor didst thou despise the persecutor[5] when he was converted. But all who came to thee in repentance thou didst reckon among thy friends: Thou alone who art blessed, now, and world without end. Amen.

10. *Another Prayer of S. John Chrysostom*

O LORD JESUS CHRIST, my God, absolve, remit, cleanse and forgive me, thy sinful, unprofitable[6] and unworthy servant, my sins, offences and transgressions, which from my youth even unto this present day and hour I have sinned against thee, witting or unwitting, whether of word or deed, whether in thought or imagination, in my own counsels[7] and in all my senses. And by the prayers of her who bare thee, Mary, thy most pure and ever-Virgin Mother, my hope which maketh not ashamed,[8] my support and my salvation, vouchsafe that I may partake without condemnation of thy most holy, immortal, life-giving and dread mysteries, for the remission of sins[9] and unto life eternal; unto hallowing and enlightning, unto strength, healing and health of soul and body; and unto the destruction and dispatch of my perverse thoughts and imaginings and intents, of night phantoms and the evil spirits of darkness; For thine is the kingdom, the power and the glory, the honour and worship, with the Father and thy Holy Spirit, now, and for ever: world without end. Amen.

---

[1] Matt. 8: 8.   [2] Luke 7: 37.   [3] Luke 18: 13.   [4] Luke 23: 42.   [5] Acts 9: vv. 4–6.
[6] Matt. 25: 30.   [7] Ps. 81: 12.   [8] Rom. 5: 5.   [9] Matt. 26: 28.

11. *A Prayer of S. John Damascene*

Though I stand before the doors of thy temple, yet I refrain not from my evil thoughts. But thou, O CHRIST my GOD, didst justify the publican,[1] and shew mercy upon the woman of Canaan,[2] and open the gates of paradise to the thief:[3] Open unto me the bowels of thy loving-kindness,[4] and accept thou me, who would approach unto thee and would feel thee, as thou didst accept the woman in the city, and her with the issue of blood: for the one having touched the hem of thy garment was readily made whole; the other who washed thy feet with tears was forgiven her sins.[5] And I, a pitiful wretch, make bold to receive thy whole body, yet let me not be consumed. And reject me not, even as thou didst not reject them; And enlighten my spiritual senses, and consume the guilt of my sins, through the prayers of her who without seed gave birth to thee, and of the heavenly hosts: For blessed art thou unto ages of ages. Amen.

12. *A Prayer of S. John Chrysostom*

I believe, O LORD, and confess that thou art in truth the Christ, the Son of the living God,[6] come into the world to save sinners; of whom I am chief.[7] And I believe that this is indeed thine incorruptible body, and this thy most precious blood. Wherefore I pray thee, have mercy upon me, and forgive me my trespasses, voluntary and involuntary, whether of word or deed, witting or unwitting; And vouchsafe that I may partake without condemnation of thy most pure mysteries, for the remission of sins[8] and unto life everlasting. Amen.

And making ready to partake of the sacred gifts pronounce in thy heart this versicle from

S. Simeon Metaphrastes

Behold I draw near to divine Communion,
O Creator, let me not be destroyed thereby;
For thou art fire to consume the unworthy.
The rather do thou cleanse me from all that defileth.

---

[1] Luke 18: 14.   [2] Matt. 15: vv. 22–8.   [3] Luke 23: 43.   [4] Phil. 2: 1; Col. 3: 12.
[5] Matt. 9: vv. 20–2; Luke 8: vv. 43–8; Luke 7: vv. 37–48.   [6] Matt. 16: 16.   [7] 1 Tim. 1: 15.
[8] Matt. 26: 28.

This also say

Of thy mystical supper, O Son of God, accept me this day as a partaker; For I will not speak of the mystery to thine enemies, nor will I give thee a kiss like Judas;[1] but like the thief I will acknowledge thee: Remember me, O Lord, in thy Kingdom.[2]

And these lines

The blood that maketh divine, O man,
Let it be your fear, let it be your dread.[3]
Fire it is to consume the unworthy.
The divine body doth make me
A partaker of the divine nature,[4]
And likewise feedeth me.
Maketh the spirit divine
And wondrously[5] nourisheth[6] the mind.

Likewise the troparia

Thou hast ravished my heart[7] with thy love, O Christ,
Thy divine care hath converted my soul.[8]
Yet do thou consume my sins with celestial[9] fire.[10]
And grant me to delight myself in thee;[11]
That rejoicing I may exalt[12]
Thine incarnation and thy second coming,
O thou who art good.

How may I, unworthy as I am,
Enter into the brightness of thy saints?
For if I come boldly to the king's palace
My apparel doth convict me,
In that I have no wedding garment,
And I shall be bound and cast away by the angels.[13]
O Lord, cleanse my soul from all filthiness,[14]
And save me[15] for thou art loving-kind.

---

[1] Matt. 26: 49; Mark 14: 45.   [2] Luke 23: 42.   [3] Isa. 8: 13.   [4] 2 Pet. 1: 4.   [5] Joel 2: 26.
[6] Gen. 45: 11.   [7] Song of Solomon 4: 9.   [8] Ps. 19: 7.   [9] 1 Cor. 15: 40.   [10] Deut. 4: 24.
[11] Isa. 58: 14.   [12] Isa. 25: 1.   [13] Matt. 22: vv. 11–13; Matt. 13: vv. 41–2.   [14] 2 Cor. 7: 1.
[15] Matt. 14: 30.

And the Prayer

O MASTER and LOVER of mankind, LORD JESUS CHRIST, my GOD, let not these holy things[1] be to my judgment, in that I am unworthy: but rather unto the cleansing and hallowing of soul and body, unto an earnest[2] of life eternal and the Kingdom. For I hold it good to cleave to God,[3] to hope in the Lord for my salvation.[4]

And this

Of thy mystical supper, O Son of God, accept me this day as a par-taker; For I will not speak of the mystery to thine enemies, nor will I give thee a kiss like Judas;[5] but like the thief I will acknowledge thee: Remember me, O Lord, in thy Kingdom.[6]

---

[1] Ezek. 22: 26.   [2] 2 Cor. 1: 22.   [3] Rom. 12: 9.   [4] Ps. 119: 166.   [5] Matt. 26: 49; Mark 14: 45.   [6] Luke 23: 42.

THE
ORDERING
OF THE
HOLY AND DIVINE
LITURGY

The Priest who would celebrate the Divine Mystery ought aforehand to be reconciled with all men and bear no ill will toward any; And so far as he is able he shall guard his heart from evil thoughts. From the evening before he shall hold himself sober and vigilant in mind and body until the hour for the Sacred Office.

THE PREPARATION OF THE MINISTERS

When the time is come the Priest shall enter the church and being joined by the Deacon together they shall bow themselves thrice to the east before the Holy Doors.

Thereupon the Deacon shall say

Master, give the blessing.

Priest

Blessed is our God always, now, and for ever:[1] world without end.[2] Amen.

The Deacon shall now begin, saying

O heavenly King and Comforter, Spirit of truth,[3] which art in all places and fillest all things; Treasure of goodness and Giver of life: Come and abide in us, and cleanse us from all that defileth. And save our souls, O Thou who art good.

O holy God, Holy and Strong, Holy and Immortal, have mercy upon us. [*thrice*]

---

[1] Isa. 26: 4. [2] Isa. 45: 17; Eph. 3: 21. [3] John 14: vv. 16–17.

Glory be to the Father, and to the Son, and to the Holy Ghost; now, and for ever: world without end. Amen.

Most Holy Trinity, have mercy upon us. O Lord, purge away our sins.[1] O Master, pardon our transgressions. O Holy One, visit and heal our infirmities, for thy name's sake.[1]

Lord, have mercy.   [*thrice*]

Glory be to the Father, and to the Son, and to the Holy Ghost; now, and for ever: world without end. Amen.

Our Father which art in heaven,[2] Hallowed be thy Name, Thy kingdom come, Thy will be done, in earth as it is in heaven. Give us this day our daily bread; And forgive us our trespasses, As we forgive them that trespass against us; And lead us not into temptation, But deliver us from evil.

Priest

For thine is the kingdom, the power, and the glory,[3] of the Father, and of the Son, and of the Holy Ghost; now, and for ever: world without end. Amen.

Then shall they say

Have mercy upon us, O Lord, have mercy upon us. Sinners bare of all defence, we lay this prayer before thee, as our Sovereign Lord. Have mercy upon us.

Glory be to the Father, and to the Son, and to the Holy Ghost.

O Lord, have mercy upon us, for in thee have we put our trust. Be not altogether wroth with us, neither remember thou our iniquities; but inasmuch as thou art merciful look down upon us at this time, and redeem us from our enemies:[4] For thou art our God and we are thy people. We all are the work of thy hand,[5] and we call upon thy name.

Now, and for ever: world without end. Amen.

O blessed Mother of God, open the gates of compassion unto us whose hope is in thee, that we be not confounded but through thee

---

[1] Ps. 79: 9.   [2] Matt. 6: vv. 9–13; Luke 11: vv. 2–4; *Book of Common Prayer*.   [3] 1 Tim. 1: 17.   [4] Ps. 136: 24.   [5] Isa. 64: 8.

be preserved from all adversity; For thou art the salvation of all Christian peoples.

Then shall they approach the ikon of Christ with reverence, saying

Unto thy most pure image, Lord, we bow, beseeching forgiveness of our sins, O Christ our God: For of thine own good will thou didst vouchsafe to ascend the cross in the flesh, that so thou mightest deliver from the bondage of the enemy them that thou didst fashion: Wherefore we cry aloud unto thee with thanksgiving. With joy hast thou filled all creation, O Saviour who didst come to save the world.

In like manner they shall turn to the ikon of the Mother of God, reciting the while the troparion

> O thou who art a fount of mercy,
> Vouchsafe unto us thy compassion.
> O Mother of God, look down upon thy sinful people.
> Make manifest thy continuing power,
> According as we hope in thee,[1]
> And hail thee blessed,
> As aforetime did Gabriel,[2] prince of the bodiless hosts.

Then shall the Priest bow his head, and say

O Lord, send thine hand[3] from thy holy habitation above, and strengthen me for this service unto thee: That without condemnation I may stand before thy dread altar, and perform the bloodless sacrifice.

For thine is the power, and the glory, for ever and ever. Amen.

THE VESTING

Then shall they bow to the congregation present and enter the sanctuary, the Priest by the south door, the Deacon by the north, saying secretly

I will enter into thine house: I will worship in thy fear toward thy holy temple.

Lead me, O Lord, in thy righteousness because of mine enemies; make my way plain before thy face. For there is no truth in their

---

[1] Ps. 33: 22. [2] Luke 1: 28. [3] Ps. 144: 7.

mouth; their heart is vain; their throat is an open sepulchre; with their tongues they have used deceit. Judge them, O God; let them fail of their counsels: cast them out according to the abundance of their ungodliness, for they have provoked thee, O Lord.

But let all that trust on thee be glad in thee: they shall exult for ever, and thou shalt dwell among them; and all that love thy name shall rejoice in thee. For thou, Lord, shalt bless the righteous: thou hast compassed us as with a shield of favour.[1]

Being come into the sanctuary they shall prostrate themselves thrice before the holy altar, and kiss the Gospel Book and the altar-table. Then each shall take his stikharion *in his right hand and make three reverences toward the east, saying each within himself*

O God, cleanse thou me a sinner, and be merciful to me.[2]

The Deacon shall now come to the Priest, holding his stikharion *in his right hand, with his* orarion, *and bowing his head to him he shall say*

Bless, Master, the *stikharion*, with the *orarion*.

Priest

Blessed is our God always, now, and for ever: world without end.

The Deacon shall go apart to one side of the sanctuary and put on his stikharion, *praying in this wise*

Let my soul rejoice in the Lord; for he has clothed me with the robe of salvation, and the garment of joy: he has put a mitre on me as on a bridegroom, and adorned me with ornaments as a bride.[3]

And kissing the orarion *he shall place it on his left shoulder. And when he fastens the cuffs around his wrists he shall say as he puts on the right cuff*

Thy right hand, O Lord, is become glorious in power: thy right hand, O Lord, hath dashed in pieces the enemy.

And in the greatness of thine excellency thou hast overthrown them that rose up against thee.[4]

---

[1] Ps. 5: vv. 7-12 (*Septuagint*, Bagster edition).   [2] Luke 18: 13.   [3] Isa. 61: 10 (*Septuagint*).
[4] Exod. 15: vv. 6-7.

And with the left he shall say

Thy hands have made me and fashioned me: give me understanding, that I may learn thy commandments.[1]

Then going to the offertory-table he shall set out the sacred vessels: the paten on the left side, the chalice, which is the holy cup, on the right, and the other holy utensils with them.

And the Priest shall vest himself on this wise: Taking his stikharion *in his left hand, and making a reverence thrice toward the east as aforesaid, he shall sign it with the sign of the cross, saying*

Blessed is our God always, now, and for ever: world without end. Amen.

Putting it on he shall say

Let my soul rejoice in the Lord; for he has clothed me with the robe of salvation, and the garment of joy: he has put a mitre on me as on a bridegroom, and adorned me with ornaments as a bride.[2]

Then taking his epitrakhelion *he shall sign it with the sign of the cross and put it about his neck, saying*

Blessed is God who poureth out his grace upon his priests, like the precious ointment upon the head, that ran down upon the beard, even Aaron's beard: that went down to the skirts of his garments.[3]

Likewise taking the zone *and girding himself therewith he shall say*

Blessed is God that girdeth me with strength, and maketh my way perfect.
   He maketh my feet like hinds' feet, and setteth me upon my high places.[4]

Putting on the cuffs he shall say as was directed above.

---

[1] Ps. 119: 73.   [2] Isa. 61: 10 (*Septuagint*).   [3] Ps. 133: 2.   [4] Ps. 18: vv. 32–3.

Then taking his epigonation, *if he has that dignity, he shall bless it and kiss it, saying*

Gird thy sword upon thy thigh, O most mighty, with thy glory and thy majesty.

And in thy majesty ride prosperously because of truth and meekness and righteousness; and thy right hand shall teach thee terrible things:[1]

Always, now, and for ever: world without end. Amen.

Then he shall take the phelonion *and blessing and kissing it shall vest himself, saying*

Let thy priests be clothed with righteousness, O Lord; and let thy saints shout for joy:[2]

Always, now, and for ever: world without end. Amen.

Then Priest and Deacon shall go to the piscina, the where each shall wash his hands, saying

I will wash mine hands in innocency: so will I compass thine altar, O Lord:

That I may publish with the voice of thanksgiving, and tell of all thy wondrous works.

Lord, I have loved the habitation of thy house, and the place where thine honour dwelleth.

Gather not my soul with sinners, nor my life with bloody men:

In whose hands is mischief, and their right hand is full of bribes.

But as for me, I will walk in mine integrity: redeem me, and be merciful unto me.

My foot standeth in an even place: in the congregations will I bless the Lord.[3]

And so they go to the offertory-table.

---

[1] Ps. 45: vv. 3–4.   [2] Ps. 132: 9.   [3] Ps. 26: vv. 6–12.

THE *PROTHESIS*

Then making three lowly reverences before the offertory-table each shall say within himself

O God, cleanse thou me a sinner, and be merciful to me.[1]

And the Priest shall say

Thou hast redeemed us by thy precious blood from the curse of the law:[2] being nailed to the cross and pierced with the spear, thou art become for men the fount of immortal life: our Saviour, glory be to thee.

Then shall the Deacon say

Master, give the blessing.

And the Priest shall begin the

Office of Oblation

Blessed is our God always, now, and for ever: world without end.

Deacon

Amen.

Then shall the Priest take in his left hand a prosphoron, *and in his right hand the holy spear and therewith thrice making the sign of the cross over it shall say three times*

In remembrance of our Lord and God and Saviour Jesus Christ.

And immediately he shall thrust the spear into the right side of the seal, and the while he cuts it he shall say

He was led as a sheep to the slaughter.[3]

And the while he cuts the left side

And as a lamb without blemish before the shearer is dumb, so he opens not his mouth.[3]

---

[1] Luke 18: 13.   [2] Gal. 3: 13.   [3] Isa. 53: vv. 7–8 (*Septuagint*); Acts 8: vv. 32–3; 1 Pet. 1: 19.

And cutting the upper part of the seal

In his humiliation his judgment was taken away.[1]

And into the lower part, saying

Who shall declare his generation?[1]

And the Deacon reverently witnessing this mystery, at each incision shall say, holding his orarion *in his hand*

Let us pray unto the Lord.

Thereafter he shall say

Master, lift out.

And the Priest thrusting the sacred spear into the right side of the prosphoron *shall lift out the holy bread, saying*

For his life is taken away from the earth.[1]

And having laid it with the seal downwards on the paten, and the Deacon having said

Master, sacrifice,

the Priest shall cut it crosswise, saying the while

The Lamb of God, which taketh away the sin of the world[2] **is sacrificed for the life**[3] **and salvation of the world.**

And the Priest having turned the bread so that the emblem of the cross is now upward the Deacon shall say

Master, pierce.

And the Priest shall pierce the right side with the spear, saying

One of the soldiers with a spear pierced his side, and forthwith came there out blood and water.
    And he that saw it bare record, and his record is true.[4]

Then the Deacon shall take of the wine and the water, and say to the Priest

Bless, Master, the holy blending.

---

[1] Isa. 53: vv. 7–8 (*Septuagint*); Acts 8: vv. 32–3; 1 Pet. 1: 19.   [2] John 1: 29.   [3] John 6: 51.
[4] John 19: vv. 34–5.

And receiving the blessing upon them he shall pour into the chalice wine and water together

    The Priest taking in his hand a second prosphoron *shall say*

In honour and remembrance of our most blessed Lady, Mother of God and ever-Virgin Mary; at whose intercessions do thou, O Lord, accept this sacrifice unto thy heavenly altar.

And taking out a particle he shall lay it on the right side of the holy bread near the centre thereof, saying

The queen stood by on thy right hand, clothed in vesture wrought with gold, and arrayed in divers colours.[1]

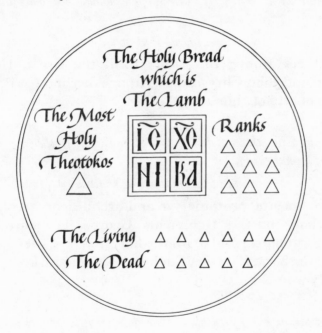

   Then taking the third prosphoron *he shall say*

Of the glorious prophet and forerunner John the Baptist.

And taking out a first particle he shall lay it on the left side of the holy bread, beginning with it the first rank.

---

[1] Ps. 44: 9 (*Septuagint*).

And he shall say

Of the holy and glorious prophets Moses and Aaron, Elijah and Elisha, David and Jesse; Of the Three Holy Children and Daniel the prophet; And of all holy prophets.

And taking out another particle he shall set it in order below the first.

And he shall say

Of the holy and all glorious apostles Peter and Paul; And of all the holy apostles.

And in like manner he shall set a third particle below the second, thus completing the first rank.

And he shall say

Of our fathers among the saints Basil the Great, Gregory the Theologian and John Chrysostom; Athanasius and Cyril, Nikolas of Myra; And of all holy hierarchs.

And taking out a fourth particle he shall place it next to the first particle, thus beginning the second rank.

And in like manner he shall say

Of the holy apostle, protomartyr and archdeacon Stephen; Of the great and holy martyrs Demetrius, George, Theodore Tiron and Theodore Stratelates; And of all the holy martyrs, men and women; Of Thekla, Barbara, Kyriaka, Euphemia, and Paraskeva, Ekaterina, and all holy women.

And taking out a fifth particle he shall set it below the fourth.

And he shall say

Of our sacred fathers whom God inspired, Antony, Euthymius, Saba, Onuphrius, Athanasius of Athos, Antony and Theodosius of Pechersk, Sergius of Radonezh, Seraphim of Sarov; And of all holy ascetics, men and women.

And in like manner taking out a sixth particle he shall place it below the fifth, thus completing the second rank.

After which he shall say

Of the holy and selfless physicians Cosmas and Damian, Cyrus and John, Panteleimon and Hermolaus; And of all holy physicians.

And taking out a seventh particle he shall place it at the top, thus beginning the third rank.

Again he shall say

Of the holy and righteous progenitors of God Joachim and Anna; of N. [*the saint to whom the church is dedicated*]; **and of N.** [*the saint to whose memory the day is dedicated*]; **And of all the saints, at whose intercessions visit us, O Lord.**

And he shall set an eighth particle in order below the seventh.

And thereafter he shall pray

Of our father among the saints John Chrysostom, archbishop of Constantinople. [*But if the Liturgy of S. Basil the Great is to be celebrated, then* **Basil the Great, archbishop of Caesaria in Cappadocia** *shall be commemorated instead*]

And so taking a ninth particle he shall set it below the eighth particle, to complete the third rank.

Then taking a fourth prosphoron *he shall say*

Remember, O Lord, all the Orthodox episcopate; Our most holy Patriarch N., the honourable order of priesthood, the diaconate which is in Christ, and all the clergy; Our brethren and fellow-ministers, the priests, the deacons and all our brotherhood which thou hast called into thy fellowship, by thy tender mercy, O gracious Sovereign.

And taking out a particle he shall lay it below the holy bread.

Then he shall commemorate those of the living whose names he hath, and at each name he shall take out a particle, saying

Remember, O Lord, N.

And having thus taken out the particles he shall place them below the holy bread.

Then taking a fifth prosphoron *he shall say*

For a remembrance and in remission of the sins of the blessed founders of this holy temple.

Then he shall commemorate the bishop who ordained him, and such of those that have departed this life, as he will, and at each name he shall separate a particle saying

Remember, O Lord, N.

And lastly he shall say thus

And all our Orthodox fathers and brethren, fallen asleep in the hope of resurrection, of life eternal and fellowship with thee, O Lord, who dost love mankind.

And he shall take out a particle.

Thereupon he shall say

Remember, O Lord, my sinful self, and forgive me my trespasses, voluntary and involuntary.

And he shall take out a particle.

And with the spunge he shall gather the particles below the holy bread upon the paten, that all be secure and none may fall.

The Deacon then taking the censer and putting incense therein shall say to the Priest

Master, bless the incense.

And straightway

Let us pray unto the Lord.

And the Priest shall say the prayer for the blessing of incense

We offer incense unto thee, O Christ our God, for a sweetsmelling savour[1] of spiritual fragrance, which do thou accept upon thy most heavenly altar; And send down upon us the grace of thy most holy Spirit.

Deacon

Let us pray unto the Lord.

---

[1] Eph. 5: 2.

Then the Priest shall cense the asterisk *and set it over the holy bread saying*

And the star came and stood over where the young child was.[1]

Deacon

Let us pray unto the Lord.

Censing the first veil the Priest shall cover therewith the holy bread and the paten saying

The Lord reigneth, he is clothed with majesty; the Lord is clothed with strength, wherewith he hath girded himself: the world also is stablished, that it cannot be moved.

Thy throne is established of old: thou art from everlasting.

The floods have lifted up, O Lord, the floods have lifted up their voice; the floods lift up their waves.

The Lord on high is mightier than the noise of many waters, yea, than the mighty waves of the sea.

Thy testimonies are very sure: holiness becometh thine house, O Lord, for ever.[2]

Deacon

Let us pray unto the Lord. Master, cover with the veil.

The Priest shall then cense the second veil and cover the chalice saying

Thy virtue, O Christ, covered the heavens, and the earth was full of thy praise.[3]

Deacon

Let us pray unto the Lord. Master, cover with the veil.

The Priest shall cense the third veil, that is the aer, *and cover both (the paten and the chalice) saying*

Hide us under the shadow of thy wings,[4] **and drive from us every foe and adversary. Grant us a peaceable life, O Lord. Have mercy upon us, and upon thy world. And save our souls, for thou art good and lovingkind.**

---

[1] Matt. 2: 9.   [2] Ps. 93.   [3] Hab. 3: 3.   [4] Ps. 17: 8.

Then taking the censer the Priest shall cense the whole oblation, repeating thrice

Blessed is our God, who hath been well pleased[1] on this wise. Glory be unto thee.

And each time the Deacon shall respond

Always, now, and for ever: world without end. Amen.

And both shall make three devout reverences. And the Deacon taking the censer shall say

For the precious gifts here set forth, let us pray unto the Lord.

And the Priest shall begin

The Prayer of Oblation

O God, our God, who didst send the bread which cometh down from heaven and giveth food to all flesh,[2] Jesus Christ, our Lord and God, our Saviour, Redeemer[3] and Benefactor, by whom we are hallowed and blessed: Do thou bless this oblation here set forth, and receive it unto thy most heavenly altar. Remember of thy goodness and lovingkindness them by whom and for whom these things are offered; And preserve us uncondemned in the sacred service of thy divine mysteries.

For hallowed and glorified is thy sublime and wondrous name, of the Father, and of the Son, and of the Holy Ghost; now, and for ever: world without end. Amen.

Whereupon he shall pronounce a Dismissal saying

Glory be unto thee, O Christ our God and our hope,[4] glory be unto thee.

Deacon

Glory be to the Father, and to the Son, and to the Holy Ghost; now, and for ever: world without end. Amen.

Lord, have mercy.   [*thrice*]

Master, give the blessing.

---

[1] Isa. 42: 21.   [2] Ps. 136: 25.   [3] Isa. 60: 16.   [4] I Tim. 1: 1.

The Priest shall pronounce the Dismissal

May Christ our true God, [*if it be a Sunday* who is risen from the dead,] by the prayers of his most holy Mother; of our father among the saints, John Chrysostom, archbishop of Constantinople; [*or if the Liturgy of S. Basil the Great is to be celebrated, then* Basil the Great, archbishop of Caesarea in Cappadocia;] and of all the saints, have mercy upon us, and save our souls: For he is good and loving-kind.

Deacon

Amen.

THE CENSING

After the Dismissal the Deacon shall cense the holy prothesis. *Then he shall go to cense the sacred altar round about, in the form of a cross, saying secretly*

> In the tomb according to the flesh,
> As God in hell with the soul,
> In paradise with the thief,
> And on the throne with the Father and the Spirit
> Wast thou, O Christ, omnipresent, incircumscript.

And then **Psalm 51**

Have mercy upon me, O God, according to thy lovingkindness: according unto the multitude of thy tender mercies blot out my transgressions.

Wash me throughly from mine iniquity, and cleanse me from my sin.

For I acknowledge my transgressions: and my sin is ever before me.

Against thee, thee only, have I sinned, and done this evil in thy sight: that thou mightest be justified when thou speakest, and be clear when thou judgest.

Behold, I was shapen in iniquity; and in sin did my mother conceive me.

Behold, thou desirest truth in the inward parts: and in the hidden part thou shall make me to know wisdom.

Purge me with hyssop, and I shall be clean: wash me, and I shall be whiter than snow.

Make me to hear joy and gladness; that the bones which thou hast broken may rejoice.

Hide thy face from my sins, and blot out all mine iniquities.

Create in me a clean heart, O God; and renew a right spirit within me.

Cast me not away from thy presence; and take not thy holy spirit from me.

Restore unto me the joy of thy salvation; and uphold me with thy free spirit.

Then will I teach transgressors thy ways; and sinners shall be converted unto thee.

Deliver me from bloodguiltiness, O God, thou God of my salvation: and my tongue shall sing aloud of thy righteousness.

O Lord, open thou my lips; and my mouth shall shew forth thy praise.

For thou desirest not sacrifice; else would I give it: thou delightest not in burnt offering.

The sacrifices of God are a broken spirit: a broken and a contrite heart, O God, thou wilt not despise.

Do good in thy good pleasure unto Zion: build thou the walls of Jerusalem.

Then shalt thou be pleased with the sacrifices of righteousness, with burnt offering and whole burnt offering: then shall they offer bullocks upon thine altar.

And meanwhile he shall cense the sanctuary and all the temple, and shall return to the sanctuary to cense the holy altar and the Priest, before laying the censer aside in its place and joining the Priest.

THE FINAL PREPARATION

And standing together before the holy table the Priest and the Deacon shall bow themselves thrice, each praying within himself and saying

O heavenly King and Comforter, Spirit of truth, which art in all places and fillest all things; Treasure of goodness and Giver of life: Come and abide in us, and cleanse us from all that defileth. And save our souls, O thou who art good.

Glory to God in the highest, and on earth peace, good will toward men.[1] [*twice*]

O Lord, open thou my lips; and my mouth shall shew forth thy praise.[2]

The Priest shall then kiss the Book of the Holy Gospels, and the Deacon the holy table. Thereupon the Deacon bowing his head before the Priest and holding his orarion with three fingers of his right hand shall say

It is time for thee, Lord, to work.[3]

Master, give the blessing.

The Priest shall make the sign of the cross over him saying

Blessed is our God always, now, and for ever: world without end.

Deacon

Pray for me, holy Master.

Priest

The Lord direct thy steps.[4]

Deacon

Remember me, holy Master.

Priest

The Lord God remember thee in his kingdom always, now, and for ever: world without end.

Deacon

Amen.

And having made a humble reverence the Deacon shall leave the sanctuary by the north door, for the Holy Doors are not opened until the Entrance.

---

[1] Luke 2: 14.   [2] Ps. 51: 15.   [3] Ps. 119: 126.   [4] Prov. 16: 9.

THE *ENARXIS*

And standing in his accustomed place before the Holy Doors the Deacon shall bow himself reverently thrice, saying secretly

O Lord, open thou my lips; and my mouth shall shew forth thy praise.[1]

And thereupon he shall begin

Master, give the blessing.

Priest

Blessed is the kingdom . . .
[*and the rest as below*]

---

[1] Ps. 51: 15.

NOTE. *If the priest shall minister without a deacon he shall not say on his account the words appointed to the deacon in the Office of Oblation; or in the liturgy before the Gospel; nor 'Master, give the blessing'; nor 'Master, sacrifice'; nor 'It is time for thee, Lord, to work'; but only the litanies and oblation as prescribed to him.*

And in cathedral churches where many priests minister, only one priest shall perform the Office of Oblation, and say what is herein set forth. And none of the priests shall say that Office separately.

THE
DIVINE LITURGY
OF OUR FATHER AMONG THE SAINTS
JOHN CHRYSOSTOM

THE LITURGY OF THE CATECHUMENS

THE *ENARXIS*

Deacon

Master, give the blessing.

Priest

BLESSED is the kingdom of the Father, and of the Son, and of the Holy Ghost; now, and for ever: world without end.

Deacon

In peace let us pray unto the Lord,

For the peace from on high, and for the salvation of our souls, let us pray unto the Lord,

For the peace and union of the whole world, and for the good estate of the holy churches of God, let us pray unto the Lord,

For this holy temple and for them that enter therein with faith, reverence and fear of God, let us pray unto the Lord,

Choir

Amen

*Kyrie eleison**

---

* The Choir shall sing *Kyrie eleison* after each petition.

Choir

For our Patriarch *N.*; for the honourable order of priesthood; and for the diaconate which is in Christ; For all the clergy and the people, let us pray unto the Lord,

For our Sovereign Lady, Queen Elizabeth [*or the Civil Authority*]; For this country, and for those in authority over us, let us pray unto the Lord,

For this city [*or* monastery]; For every city and land, and for them that dwell therein with faith, let us pray unto the Lord,

For fair seasons and for an abundance of the fruits of the earth, let us pray unto the Lord,

For them that travel by land, by water, by air; For the sick and the suffering; For those in captivity, And for their salvation, let us pray unto the Lord,

That we may be delivered from all tribulation, wrath, danger and necessity, let us pray unto the Lord,

Succour, save, comfort and preserve us, O God, by thy grace,

Mindful of our most holy and undefiled,[1] most blessed and glorious Lady, Mother of God and ever-Virgin Mary; and of all the saints; Let us commend ourselves, and one another, and our whole life to Christ our God,

To thee, O Lord

---

[1] Heb. 7: 26.

Priest	Choir

Priest

The Prayer of the First Antiphon*

O Lord our God, whose might is ineffable; Whose glory passeth all understanding; Whose mercy is infinite; Whose love toward mankind is beyond utterance: Do thou, O Sovereign Lord, of thy compassion look down upon us, and upon this holy temple; And bestow upon us, and upon them that now make their supplications with us, thy bountiful goodness and mercy.

For unto thee belong all glory, honour and worship, unto the Father, and unto the Son, and unto the Holy Ghost; now, and for ever: world without end.

At the beginning of the antiphon the Deacon shall bow himself and go from his place to stand before the ikon of Christ, holding his orarion *with three fingers of his right hand.*

Choir

Amen

Bless the Lord, O my soul. Blessed art thou, O Lord.[1]

Bless the Lord, O my soul: and all that is within me, bless his holy name.

Bless the Lord, O my soul, and forget not all his benefits:

Who forgiveth all thine iniquities; who healeth all thy diseases;

The Lord is merciful and gracious, slow to anger, and plenteous in mercy.

---

* *Prayers that are indented and marked with a vertical line on the left, the Priest may pronounce silently or aloud, in accordance with local custom.*

[1] Ps. 119: 12.

When the antiphon is done he returneth to his accustomed place to begin the Short Litany.

Choir

Bless the Lord, O my soul: and all that is within me, bless his holy name.[1]

Blessed art thou, O Lord.

Deacon

Again and again in peace let us pray unto the Lord,

Succour, save, comfort and preserve us, O God, by thy grace,

Mindful of our most holy and undefiled, most blessed and glorious Lady, Mother of God and ever-Virgin Mary; and of all the saints; Let us commend ourselves, and one another, and our whole life to Christ our God,

Kyrie eleison

To thee, O Lord

Priest

The Prayer of the Second Antiphon

O Lord our God, save thy people, and bless thine inheritance.[2] Preserve the fulness of thy Church. Sanctify them that love the habitation of thy house.[3] Do thou by thy divine power exalt them unto glory; and forsake us not who put our trust in thee.

For thine is the might, thine the kingdom, the power and the glory, of the Father, and of the Son, and of the Holy Ghost; now, and for ever: world without end.

Amen

---

[1] Ps. 103: vv. 1–3, and v. 8. (*The whole Psalm may be sung.*)   [2] Ps. 28: 9.   [3] Ps. 26: 8.

Choir

Glory be to the Father, and to the Son, and to the Holy Ghost.

Praise the Lord, O my soul.

While I live will I praise the Lord: I will sing praises unto my God while I have any being.

Put not your trust in princes, nor in the son of man, in whom there is no help.

His breath goeth forth, he returneth to his earth; in that very day his thoughts perish.

The Lord shall reign for ever, even thy God, O Zion, unto all generations.[1]

Now, and for ever: world without end. Amen.

O only-begotten Son and Word of God, O thou who art immortal, yet for our salvation didst deign to be incarnate of the holy Mother of God and ever-Virgin Mary, and without change wast made man; Who also wast crucified for us, and by death didst overcome death: Save us, O Christ our God, One Person of the Holy Trinity, glorified together with the Father and the Holy Ghost.

Again, the while the antiphon is singing the Deacon shall go to stand before the ikon of Christ, holding his orarion *with three fingers of his right hand.*

When the antiphon is done he returneth to his accustomed place and crieth aloud

Deacon

Again and again in peace let us pray unto the Lord,

Kyrie eleison

---

[1] Ps. 146: vv. 1–4, and v. 10. (*The whole Psalm may be sung.*)

Succour, save, comfort and preserve us, O God, by thy grace,

Mindful of our most holy and undefiled, most blessed and glorious Lady, Mother of God and ever-Virgin Mary; and of all the saints; Let us commend ourselves, and one another, and our whole life to Christ our God,

Choir

To thee, O Lord

Priest

The Prayer of the Third Antiphon

O Thou who hast given us grace with one accord to make our common supplications unto thee; And dost promise that when two or three are gathered together in thy name thou wilt grant their requests: Fulfil now, O Lord, the petitions of thy servants, as may be most expedient for them; granting us in this world knowledge of thy truth, and in the world to come life everlasting.

For thou, O God, art good and loving-kind, and we ascribe glory to thee, to the Father, and to the Son, and to the Holy Ghost; now, and for ever: world without end.

Amen

In thy kingdom remember us, Lord, when thou comest into thy kingdom.[1]

---

[1] Luke 23: 42.

Choir

Blessed are the poor in spirit: for their's is the kingdom of heaven.

Blessed are they that mourn: for they shall be comforted.

Blessed are the meek: for they shall inherit the earth.

Blessed are they which do hunger and thirst after righteousness: for they shall be filled.

Blessed are the merciful: for they shall obtain mercy.

Blessed are the pure in heart: for they shall see God.

Blessed are the peacemakers: for they shall be called the children of God.

Blessed are they which are persecuted for righteousness' sake: for their's is the kingdom of heaven.

Blessed are ye, when men shall revile you, and persecute you, and shall say all manner of evil against you falsely, for my sake.

Rejoice, and be exceeding glad: for great is your reward in heaven.[1]

Glory be to the Father, and to the Son, and to the Holy Ghost; now, and for ever: world without end. Amen.

---

[1] Matt. 5: vv. 3–12.

THE LITTLE ENTRANCE

Here the Holy Doors are opened for the Little Entrance (of the Holy Gospel).

As the Choir begins the Gloria *at the end of the Beatitudes the Priest and the Deacon standing before the altar-table shall bow themselves thrice.*

The Priest shall then take the Gospel Book and give it to the Deacon, and they shall pass behind the altar and go out at the north side, preceded by lighted tapers, to make the Little Entrance.

And standing in their customary places both shall bow their heads, and the Deacon shall say

Let us pray unto the Lord,

while the Priest prays

The Prayer of the Little Entrance

O Master and Lord our God, who stablished the heavenly orders and hosts of angels and archangels to minister unto thy glory: Grant that the holy angels may enter with our entrance, to minister with us, and with us to glorify thy goodness.

For unto thee belong all glory, honour and worship, unto the Father, and unto the Son, and unto the Holy Spirit; now, and for ever: world without end. Amen.

When the prayer is finished the Deacon holding his orarion *with three fingers of his right hand and pointing therewith to the east shall say to the Priest*

| **Master, bless the holy entrance.**

And the Priest giving the benediction shall say

| **Blessed is the entrance into the holiest,[1] always, now, and for ever: world without end.**

Then the Deacon having held up the Book of the Gospels for the Priest to kiss shall come to the centre of the Holy Doors and there standing in front of the Priest he shall raise his hands somewhat and shew the Holy Gospel, and shall cry in a loud voice

Wisdom. Stand steadfast.

He shall then make a reverence and lead the Priest into the sanctuary where he shall lay the Gospel Book upon the altar, the while the Choir sings

Choir

O come, let us worship and bow down[2] before Christ.

O Son of God, [*if it be a Sunday* **who art risen from the dead,**[3]] **save us, who sing unto thee: Alleluia.**

And the customary troparia

---

[1] Heb. 10: 19.   [2] Ps. 95: 6.   [3] *On other days:* **who art wonderful in the saints**

Priest	*Choir*

The Prayer of the Trisagion

O Holy God, who restest in the holies;[1] unto whom the seraphim sing the thrice-holy song;[2] Whom the cherubim glorify, and all the heavenly hosts adore; Who didst bring into being all that exists; Who didst create man in thine own image and likeness,[3] and didst adorn him with thine every gift; Who givest wisdom and understanding to him that asketh, and art not wroth with the sinner,[4] but dost grant repentance to salvation;[5] Who hast deemed us, thine humble and unmeritable servants, worthy at this hour to stand before the glory of thy holy altar, to bring unto thee rightful worship and praise: Accept, O Master, from the mouths of us sinners the thrice-holy hymn, and visit us with thy goodness. Pardon our offences, voluntary and involuntary. Sanctify our souls and bodies, and grant us to serve thee in holiness, all the days of our life.[6] By the prayers of the holy Mother of God, and of all the saints which have been wellpleasing unto thee since the world began.

---

[1] Isa. 57: 15 (*Septuagint*).   [2] Isa. 6: 3.   [3] Gen. 1: vv. 26–7.   [4] Isa. 54: vv. 8–9.
[5] 2 Cor. 7: 10.   [6] Luke 1: vv. 74–5.

And when the Choir comes to the last hymn the Deacon shall say to the Priest as both bow their heads and he lifts his orarion with three fingers

| **Bless, Master, the time of the Thrice-holy.**

The Priest making the sign of the cross over him shall say

For thou our God art holy, and to thee we ascribe glory, to the Father, and to the Son, and to the Holy Spirit; now, and for ever:

And when the hymn is ended the Deacon shall come close to the Holy Doors and pointing with his orarion *to the ikon of Christ he shall say,*

| **O Lord save the faithful, and give ear unto us.**

Then turning to them that stand without he shall cry aloud

And world without end.

Choir

Amen
O Holy God, Holy and Strong, Holy and Immortal, have mercy upon us.   *[thrice]*

Glory be to the Father, and to the Son, and to the Holy Ghost; now, and for ever: world without end. Amen.

Holy and Immortal, have mercy upon us.

The Priest and the Deacon the while repeat the Thrice-holy secretly and together bow themselves thrice before the holy altar,* and the Deacon shall say to the Priest

| **Thy bidding, Master.**

---

* *Here shall follow the Consecrating of a Bishop.*

And they shall proceed toward the throne, the Priest saying as he goes

| Blessed is he that cometh in the name of the Lord.[1]

Choir

O Holy God, Holy and Strong, Holy and Immortal, have mercy upon us.

Deacon

| Bless, Master, the throne on high.

Priest

| Blessed art thou on the glorious throne of thy kingdom, that sittest upon the cherubim;[2] always, now, and for ever: world without end.

It is to be observed that the Priest is not himself to ascend the throne or sit thereon: but to sit on the south side thereof.

THE LESSON

And after the conclusion of the Tri-sagion the Deacon shall come before the Holy Doors and shall say

Let us give heed.

Priest

Peace unto all.

Reader

And unto thy spirit.

---

[1] Ps. 118: 26; Matt. 21: 9; Mark 11: 9; Luke 13: 35.　　[2] Song of the 3 Childr. vv. 33, 32.

Deacon	*Choir*

Wisdom.

The reader then reads the prokhimenon

Deacon

Wisdom.

Reader

The reading is from the [Acts of the Apostles *or* **Epistle of Paul the Apostle to . . .** *or* **First/Second Epistle General of . . .]**

Deacon

Let us give heed.

The reader then reads the Lesson

Brethren, . . .

And when the Epistle is finished the Priest shall say

Peace unto thee that readest.

Reader

And unto thy spirit.

Deacon

Wisdom.

Reader

Alleluia. Alleluia. Alleluia.

During the singing of the Alleluia *the Deacon shall take the censer with the incense, and approaching the Priest shall receive his blessing. And shall thereafter cense the holy altar round about, and all the sanctuary, and the Priest.*

Now the Priest standing before the holy table shall say this prayer

The Prayer before the Gospel

O Lord and lover of mankind: Make the imperishable light of thy divine knowledge to shine in our hearts; And open the eyes of our understanding[1] that we may apprehend the preaching of thy Gospel. Implant in us likewise awe of thy blessed commandments, that trampling under feet[2] all the lusts of the flesh we may pursue a spiritual life, thinking and doing always such things as are pleasing in thy sight;[3] For thou art the enlightning of our souls and bodies, O Christ our God, and unto thee we render glory, together with thine eternal Father and thine all holy, gracious and life-giving Spirit; now, and for ever: world without end. Amen.

The Deacon having put aside the censer in its appointed place shall come to the Priest, and bowing his head to him shall point to the Book of the Gospels with his orarion, *the which he holds with the tips of his fingers, and shall say*

Bless, Master, the herald of the holy Apostle and Evangelist *N.*

Choir

---

[1] Eph. 1: 18.   [2] Ps. 91: 13.   [3] 1 John 3: 22.

The Priest signing him with the sign of the cross shall say

May God through the prayers of the holy and all glorious Apostle and Evangelist N. grant thee to preach the word with much power, unto the fulfilling of the gospel of his beloved Son, our Lord Jesus Christ.

And he shall give the Book to the Deacon.

Deacon

| **Amen.**

Then shall the Deacon do reverence to the Book of the Holy Gospels and taking it in his hands shall step forth through the Holy Doors, preceded by a tall candle which is carried before him, and go to the tribune or customary place.

Then the Priest standing before the holy altar with his face to the west shall cry in a loud voice

Wisdom. Stand steadfast. Let us hear the Holy Gospel.

Peace unto all.

Deacon

The reading is from the Holy Gospel according to N.

Priest

Let us give heed.

Choir

And unto thy spirit

Glory be to thee, O Lord, glory be to thee

[If there be two Deacons then one instead of the Priest shall proclaim **Wisdom. Stand steadfast** *and also* **Let us give heed**]

Choir

Deacon

At that time . . . [*and the reading from the Gospel*]

Which being finished the Priest shall say

Peace unto thee that dost preach the good tidings.

Glory be to thee, O Lord, glory be to thee

Then the Deacon shall go to the Holy Doors and shall deliver the Book of the Gospels to the Priest, and the Doors shall be shut again.

THE COMMON PRAYERS

Then the Deacon standing in his accustomed place shall begin the Litany following

Let us all say with our whole soul, and with our whole mind, let us say,

    O Almighty Lord, God of our fathers, we pray thee, hear and have mercy,

    Have mercy upon us, O God, after thy great goodness. We pray thee, hear and have mercy,

    We beseech thee also for our Patriarch N.; for all priests and religious; and for all our brethren in Christ,

Kyrie eleison

Kyrie eleison   [*thrice*]

We beseech thee also for our Sovereign Lady, Queen Elizabeth [*or the Civil Authority*], and for all that are in authority; That we may lead a quiet and peaceable life in all godliness and honesty,[1]

We beseech thee also for blessed and ever-memorable holy Orthodox patriarchs; for pious kings and devout queens; for the founders of this holy church [*or* monastery]; And for all thy servants who have departed this life in faith and are now at rest,

We beseech thee also for grace, life, peace, health and salvation for the servants of God *** *** ***,

We beseech thee also for them that strive[2] and bring forth the fruit of good works in this holy and venerable temple; for them that serve and them that sing; And for all the people here present who await thy great and bountiful mercy,

During the Litany the Priest shall say

The Prayer of Fervent Supplication

O Lord our God, accept this fervent supplication from thy servants, and have mercy upon us according unto the

Choir

---

[1] 1 Tim. 2: 2. [2] Phil. 1: 27.

multitude[1] of thy mercies; And
send down thy bounties upon
us and upon all thy people
which look unto thee for
plenteous mercy.[2]

Choir

For thou, O God, art gracious[3]
and full of compassion, and unto
thee we ascribe glory, unto the
Father, and unto the Son, and
unto the Holy Spirit; now, and for
ever: world without end.

Amen

*If there be a commemoration of them
that are fallen asleep the Deacon shall
say this Litany following*

Have mercy upon us, O God,
after thy great goodness. We pray
thee, hear and have mercy,

Kyrie eleison   [*thrice*]

We pray thee also for the repose of the souls of the servants
of God who have departed this
life; For *** *** ***; That they
may find pardon for all their
transgressions, voluntary and
involuntary,

That the Lord may bring their
souls to the abode of the
righteous,

For the remission of their sins;
for the mercy of God and the
kingdom of heaven: Let us entreat Christ our immortal King
and God,

Grant this, O Lord

Let us pray unto the Lord,

Kyrie eleison

---

[1] Ps. 51: 1.   [2] Ps. 86: 5; Ps. 103: 8.   [3] 1 Pet. 2: 3.

Priest

Choir

O God of spirits and of all flesh[1] which hast trodden down death and deposed the devil, and given life to thy world: Do thou, O Lord, give rest to the souls of thy servants *** *** ***, who have fallen asleep, in a place of light, in green pastures,[2] in a place of refreshing; whence pain, sorrow and mourning are fled away.[3] Every sin wrought by them in word or deed or thought, do thou pardon, as a good God and friend of man; Forasmuch as there is no man who shall live and sin not; For thou alone art without sin. Thy righteousness is an everlasting righteousness,[4] and thy word is truth:

For thou art the resurrection and the life[5] and the repose of thy departed servants *** *** ***, O Christ our God; and unto thee we ascribe glory, together with thine eternal Father, and thy most holy, good and life-giving Spirit; now, and for ever: world without end.

Amen

---

[1] Num. 16: 22 and 27: 16 (*Septuagint*).   [2] Ps. 23: 2.   [3] Isa. 51: 11.   [4] Ps. 119: 142.
[5] John 11: 25.

THE DISMISSAL OF THE CATECHUMENS

Deacon

Catechumens, pray ye unto the Lord,

Let us, the faithful, pray for the catechumens, that the Lord may have mercy upon them,

That he may instruct them in the word of truth,

That he may reveal unto them the gospel of righteousness,

That he may unite them to his Holy, Catholick and Apostolick Church,

Save them. Have mercy upon them. Protect and preserve them, O God, by thy grace,

Ye catechumens, bow your heads unto the Lord,

Choir

Kyrie eleison

To thee, O Lord

Priest

The Prayer for the Catechumens

O Lord our God who dwellest on high,[1] and dost look in mercy upon the lowly; Who for the salvation of mankind didst send forth thine only-begotten Son and God, our Lord Jesus Christ: Look in mercy upon thy servants the catechumens, who bow down before thee; And in thy good time deem them worthy of the washing of

---

[1] Ps. 113: 5.

regeneration,[1] of the remission of sins,[2] of the garment of incorruption. Unite them to thy Holy, Catholick and Apostolick Church; And number them among thy chosen flock,

That they also with us may glorify thy sublime and wondrous name, of the Father, and of the Son, and of the Holy Ghost; now, and for ever: world without end.

Choir

Amen

The Priest unfolds the antiminsion.

Deacon

All ye that are catechumens, depart.

If there be a second Deacon he also shall cry aloud

Catechumens, depart.

Then again the first Deacon

All ye catechumens, depart.
Let not any of the catechumens remain. All we the faithful, again and again in peace let us pray unto the Lord,

Kyrie eleison

---

[1] Titus 3: 5.   [2] Matt. 26: 28.

If there be but one Deacon he, or if there be no Deacon, the Priest, shall say

All ye that are catechumens, depart. Catechumens, depart. All ye catechumens, depart. Let not any of the catechumens remain. All we the faithful, again and again in peace let us pray unto the Lord,

Choir

Kyrie eleison

THE LITURGY OF THE FAITHFUL

THE PRAYERS OF THE FAITHFUL

Priest

The First Prayer of the Faithful

We give thanks unto thee, O Lord God of hosts, who hast accepted us at this time to stand at thy holy altar and bow down before thy bountiful mercy toward our sins and for the errors of the people.[1] Hear our prayer, O God. Make us worthy to bring unto thee prayers and supplications, and bloodless sacrifice for all thy people. And by the power of thy Holy Spirit enable us, whom thou hast appointed to this thy ministry, to call upon thee surely and without condemnation, at all times and in

[1] Heb. 9: 7.

all places, with the testimony of a pure conscience: That hearing us thou mayest be gracious unto us, after thy manifold goodness.

Choir

Deacon

Succour, save, comfort and preserve us, O God, by thy grace, Wisdom.

Kyrie eleison

Priest

For unto thee belong all glory, honour and worship, unto the Father, and unto the Son, and unto the Holy Ghost; now, and for ever: world without end.

Amen

Deacon

Again and again in peace let us pray unto the Lord,

Kyrie eleison

[*When the Priest celebrates without a deacon he omits the petitions here following*]

For the peace from on high, and for the salvation of our souls, let us pray unto the Lord,

For the peace and union of the whole world, and for the good estate of the holy churches of God, let us pray unto the Lord,

For this holy temple and for them that enter therein with faith, reverence and fear of God, let us pray unto the Lord,

That we may be delivered from all tribulation, wrath, danger and necessity, let us pray unto the Lord,

Choir

The Priest meanwhile shall say

The Second Prayer of the Faithful

Again and oftentimes do we incline before thee and entreat thee, O good and gracious friend of man, that thou wouldst consider our prayer and cleanse our souls and bodies from all filthiness of the flesh and spirit;[1] And suffer us to draw nigh, guiltless and without condemnation, to thy holy altar. Do thou bestow upon such also as pray with us, O God, an increase of life, and of faith, and of spiritual understanding. Vouchsafe unto them that evermore serving thee in fear and love they may partake of thy holy mysteries without guilt and without condemnation, and be deemed worthy of thy heavenly Kingdom.

Deacon

Succour, save, comfort and preserve us, O God, by thy grace, Wisdom.

Kyrie eleison

---

[1] 2 Cor. 7: 1.

Priest	Choir
That being ever guarded by thy might we may give glory to thee, to the Father, and to the Son, and to the Holy Ghost; now, and for ever: world without end.	Amen
[And the Holy Doors are opened]	

THE OFFERTORY

During the singing of the Cherubicon *the Deacon taking the censer and putting incense therein goes to the Priest and having received his blessing he shall cense the holy altar round about, and all the sanctuary, and the ikonostasis, likewise the Priest, the choir and the people, saying secretly to himself Psalm 51,* **Have mercy upon me, O God, according to thy lovingkindness;** *and other penitential* troparia *as he shall choose.*

The Priest meanwhile saith secretly

None is worthy among them that are held fast in fleshly desires and pleasures to approach thee, or draw nigh and minister unto thee, O King of glory.[1] For to minister unto thee is a great and fearful thing, even for the heavenly powers themselves. Yet do we

Let us the cherubim mystically representing, and unto the life-giving Trinity the thrice-holy chant intoning, now lay aside all earthly care.

[1] Ps. 24: vv. 7–10.

presume to serve thee forasmuch as in thine ineffable and immeasurable love toward mankind thou didst become Man, suffering thereby no change or altering, and art thyself made an high priest for us, and thyself didst bestow upon us the working of this divine office, of this bloodless sacrifice, as Master of all: For thou only, O Lord our God, hast dominion over heaven and earth, who art borne by the cherubim upon the throne, who art Lord of the seraphim and King of Israel;[1] Who only art holy and dost rest in the holies.[2]

Wherefore I make my supplication unto thee who alone art good and ready to hear. Look down upon me, thy sinful and unprofitable servant,[3] and cleanse my soul and my heart from an evil conscience.[4] And by the power of thy Holy Spirit enable me, who am invested with the grace of priesthood, to stand before this thy holy table, and to administer thy most pure and sacred body and thy precious blood. For unto thee I come, to thee I bow my head, and I beseech thee: Turn not

Choir

---

[1] John 1: 49.   [2] Isa. 57: 15 (*Septuagint*).   [3] Luke 17: 10.   [4] Heb. 10: 22.

thy face from me, neither reject me from among thy servants; but account it meet that these gifts be offered unto thee by me, thy sinful and unworthy servant. For thou art both he that offereth and he that is offered. Thou dost receive and art given, O Christ our God, and unto thee we ascribe glory, together with thine eternal Father, and thy most holy, gracious and life-giving Spirit; now, and for ever: world without end. Amen.

Choir

The prayer and the censing alike being finished, the Priest and the Deacon standing before the holy table themselves rehearse the Cherubic Hymn three times, making a reverence at the end of each repetition.

Priest

Let us the cherubim mystically representing, and unto the life-giving Trinity the thrice-holy chant intoning, now lay aside all earthly care:

Deacon

That we may raise on high the King of all, by the angelic hosts invisibly attended. Alleluia. Alleluia. Alleluia.

Then shall they proceed to the offertory-table, the Deacon going first, and the Priest shall cense the holy gifts, praying secretly the while

| O God, cleanse thou me, a sinner.

The Deacon saith unto the Priest

| Take, Master.

And the Priest taking the aer *shall lay it on the Deacon's left shoulder and shall say*

| Lift up your hands in the sanctuary, and bless the Lord.[1]

Then taking the paten he shall set it on the Deacon's head with all care and reverence, the Deacon the while holding the censer with one finger of his right hand. The chalice the Priest shall himself take in his hands, and both shall go forth at the north side, preceded by lighted tapers.

And they shall go round about the nave, each praying in turn for such as he will, at his discretion, and finally the Priest shall say

May the Lord God remember in his Kingdom you, and all faithful Christians; always, now, and for ever: world without end.

Choir

Amen

That we may raise on high the

---

[1] Ps. 134: 2.

The Deacon going in at the Holy Doors stands to the right and as the Priest enters he shall say to him

**King of all, by the angelic hosts invisibly attended.
Alleluia. Alleluia. Alleluia.**

May the Lord God remember thy priesthood in his Kingdom.

And the Priest to him

May the Lord God remember thy sacred ministry in his Kingdom; always, now, and for ever: world without end.

And the Priest shall then set the holy chalice upon the altar, and taking from the Deacon's head the holy paten he sets it down likewise, saying

Down from the tree Joseph, a godly man, took thy most pure body, and wound it in linen clothes with the spices, and laid and closed it in a new sepulchre.[1]

**In the tomb according to the flesh,
As God in hell with the soul,
In paradise with the thief,
And on the throne with the Father and the Spirit
Wast thou, O Christ, omnipresent, incircumscript.**

**Thy life-giving tomb is revealed to us
Lovelier far than paradise,**

---

[1] John 19: vv. 40–1.

More radiant than a king's palace,
O Christ, the well-spring of our resurrection.

Choir

Then shall he take the veils from the paten and the chalice, and shall lay them on one side of the holy altar; and taking the aer *from the Deacon's shoulder and censing it he shall cover therewith the holy gifts, and shall say*

Down from the tree Joseph, a godly man, took thy most pure body, and wound it in linen clothes with the spices, and laid and closed it in a new sepulchre.[1]

And taking the censer from the hands of the Deacon he shall cense the holy gifts three times, saying the while

Do good in thy good pleasure unto Zion: build thou the walls of Jerusalem.
Then shalt thou be pleased with the sacrifices of righteousness, with burnt offering and whole burnt offering: then shall they offer bullocks upon thine altar.[2]

And giving back the censer he shall bow his head and say to the Deacon

Remember me, brother and fellow-minister.

---

[1] John 19: vv. 40-1.   [2] Ps. 51: vv. 18-19.

And the Deacon shall say to him

May the Lord God remember thy priesthood in his Kingdom.

And the Deacon likewise bowing his head and holding his orarion *the while with three fingers of his right hand shall say to the Priest*

Pray for me, reverend Master.

Priest

The Holy Ghost shall come upon thee, and the power of the Highest shall overshadow thee.[1]

Deacon

The same Spirit shall labour with us all the days of our life.

And the Deacon again

Remember me, reverend Master.

Priest

The Lord God remember thee in his Kingdom; always, now, and for ever: world without end.

Deacon

Amen.

*

Choir

---

* *Here shall follow the Ordering of a Priest.*   [1] Luke 1: 35.

And having kissed the Priest's right hand he goes out at the north door and standing in his customary place he shall say

Let us complete our supplication unto the Lord,

    For the precious gifts here set forth, let us pray unto the Lord,

    For this holy temple and for them that enter therein with faith, reverence and fear of God, let us pray unto the Lord,

    That we may be delivered from all tribulation, wrath, danger and necessity, let us pray unto the Lord,

After he has set the divine gifts upon the holy altar the Priest shall pronounce

The Offertory Prayer

Lord God Almighty which only art holy; Who dost accept the sacrifice of praise from such as call upon thee with their whole heart: Accept and receive also unto thy holy altar the supplication of us sinners; And enable us to offer unto thee both gifts and spiritual sacrifices[1] for our sins and for the errors of the people.[2] And account us worthy to find grace in thy sight, that our sacrifice

Choir

Kyrie eleison

----

[1] Heb. 5: 1; 1 Pet. 2: 5.   [2] Heb. 9: 7.

may be wellpleasing to thee,[1] and the good Spirit of thy grace may dwell in us, and in these gifts here set forth; And in all thy people.

Choir

Deacon

Succour, save, comfort and preserve us, O God, by thy grace,

Kyrie eleison

That this whole day may be perfect, holy, peaceful and without sin, let us entreat the Lord,

Grant us, O Lord

For an angel of peace, faithful guide and guardian of our souls and bodies, let us entreat the Lord,

For pardon and remission of our sins and transgressions, let us entreat the Lord,

For things good and profitable to our souls, and peace for the world, let us entreat the Lord,

That we may pass the remainder of our lives in peace and repentance, let us entreat the Lord,

For a Christian ending to our life, painless, without shame and peaceful, and a good defence before the dread judgment seat of Christ,[2] let us entreat the Lord,

Mindful of our most holy and undefiled, most blessed and glorious Lady, Mother of God and ever-Virgin Mary; and of all

---

[1] Phil. 4: 18. [2] 2 Cor. 5: 10.

the saints; Let us commend ourselves and one another, and our
whole life to Christ our God,

To thee, O Lord

Priest

Through the bountiful mercies
of thine only-begotten Son, with
whom thou art blessed; together
with thy most holy, good and
life-giving Spirit; now, and for
ever: world without end.

Amen

THE KISS OF PEACE

Priest

Peace unto all.

And unto thy spirit

Deacon

Let us love one another that with
one mind we may confess

The Father, and the Son, and
the Holy Spirit, Trinity consubstantial and undivided

*And the Priest shall bow himself thrice
and say secretly within himself*

> I will love thee, O Lord, my
> strength.
>   The Lord is my rock, and my
> fortress.[1]

*And he shall kiss the holy gifts, they
being still covered: first the paten, then
the chalice and the edge of the holy
table before him. If there be two priests,
or several, they likewise shall kiss all
the holy things[2] and embrace each other
on the shoulder.*

---

[1] Ps. 18: vv. 1–2.   [2] Ezek. 22: 26.

Then the Celebrant shall say

| **Christ is in the midst of us.**

And he that has been embraced shall reply

| **He is, and ever shall be.**

The deacons also, if there be two or more, shall kiss each the cross upon his orarion *and shall embrace each other, in like manner as the priests, and repeating the same words.*

Then the Deacon shall bow himself in the place where he stands and kiss the cross upon his orarion, *and cry aloud*

The doors, the doors. In wisdom let us give heed.

Choir

THE CREED

Here the Priest shall take up the aer *and hold it over the sacred gifts. If there be several priests, each then takes hold of the* aer *and holding it above the sacred elements shall raise and lower, raise and lower it, each repeating to himself the Confession of Faith; And the people likewise.*

I BELIEVE in one God the Father Almighty, Maker of heaven and earth, And of all things visible and invisible:

And in one Lord Jesus Christ, the only-begotten Son of God, Begotten of the Father before all worlds, Light of Light, Very God

Choir

of very God, Begotten, not made, Being of one substance with the Father, By whom all things were made: Who for us men and for our salvation came down from heaven, And was incarnate of the Holy Ghost and the Virgin Mary, And was made man, And was crucified also for us under Pontius Pilate. He suffered and was buried, And the third day he rose again according to the Scriptures, And ascended into heaven, And sitteth on the right hand of the Father. And he shall come again with glory to judge both the quick and the dead: Whose kingdom shall have no end.

And in the Holy Ghost, The Lord and giver of life, Who proceedeth from the Father, Who with the Father and the Son together is worshipped and glorified, Who spake by the Prophets.

And in one Holy, Catholick and Apostolick Church. I acknowledge one Baptism for the remission of sins. And I look for the Resurrection of the dead, And the life of the world to come. Amen.

THE *ANAPHORA*

Deacon	*Choir*
Let us be upright, let us stand with fear, let us take heed to present the holy offering in peace.	The mercy of peace, the sacrifice of praise

Then the Priest lifting the aer *from the holy elements shall kiss it and lay it aside.*

And the Deacon making a reverence shall go into the sanctuary and there devoutly fan the holy things.[1] (*If there be no fan he shall use one of the veils.*)

Priest	
The grace of our Lord Jesus Christ, and the love of God the Father, and the communion of the Holy Ghost, be with you all.[2]	And with thy spirit
Let us lift up our hearts.	We lift them up unto the Lord
Let us give thanks unto the Lord.	It is meet and right so to worship the Father, and the Son, and the Holy Spirit, Trinity consubstantial and undivided.

The Priest shall now offer this Prayer

It is meet and right to sing praises unto thee, to bless thee, to magnify thee, to give thanks unto thee, to worship thee in

---

[1] Ezek. 22: 26.   [2] 2 Cor. 13: 14.

all places of thy dominion.[1] For thou art God ineffable, unknowable, invisible, incomprehensible, the same THOU ART[2] from everlasting to everlasting; Thou, and thine only-begotten Son, and thy Holy Spirit. Thou didst bring us from non-being into being; and didst raise us up that were fallen away; and left naught undone till thou hadst lifted us to heaven, and hadst bestowed upon us thy kingdom to come. For all these things we give thanks unto thee, and unto thine only-begotten Son, and unto thy Holy Spirit; for all whereof we know and whereof we know not; for benefits both manifest and hid which thou hast wrought upon us. We give thanks unto thee also for this ministry which thou dost deign to receive at our hands, albeit hosts of archangels and tens of thousands of angels wait upon thee, the many-eyed cherubim and the six-winged seraphim that soar aloft

Singing the triumphal hymn, exclaiming, crying aloud and saying

Choir

Holy, holy, holy is the Lord of Sabaoth:[3] heaven and earth are full of thy glory. Hosanna in

---

[1] Ps. 103: 22.   [2] Exod. 3: 14.   [3] Rom. 9: 29.

Choir

the highest. Blessed is he that cometh in the name of the Lord; Hosanna in the highest.[1]

Here again the Deacon taking the asterisk from off the holy paten shall make the sign of the cross over it and shall kiss it and lay it on one side. He shall then go to stand on the right side of the altar and there taking the fan in his hand shall wave it gently with all care and reverence over the sacred gifts, lest any fly or other insect settle thereon.

The Priest prayeth

And with these blessed Powers, O Sovereign Lord and friend of man, we also cry aloud and say: Holy and most holy art thou, and thine only-begotten Son, and thy Holy Spirit: Holy and most holy art thou, and excellent is thy glory,[2] who so loved thy world that thou didst give thine only-begotten Son, that whosoever believeth in him should not perish, but have everlasting life:[3] Who being come and having accomplished all that was appointed for our sakes, in the night that he was betrayed, nay, in the which he did give himself for the life of the world, took bread in his sacred, pure and spotless hands; and

---

[1] Isa. 6: 3; Matt. 21: 9; Mark 11: vv. 9–10.   [2] 2 Pet. 1: 17.   [3] John 3: 16.

when he had given thanks, and blessed and hallowed it, he brake it and gave it to his holy disciples and apostles, saying

Take, eat; this is my body which is broken for you[1] for the remission of sins.

The Deacon meanwhile holding his orarion with three fingers of his right hand shall shew the Priest the paten, and then in like manner the chalice, while the Priest saith

After the same manner also he took the cup, when he had supped, saying,[2]

Drink ye all of it; This is my blood of the new testament, which is shed for you and for many for the remission of sins.[3]

The Priest prayeth

Remembering therefore this commandment of salvation, and all those things which came to pass for our sakes: the cross, the tomb, the resurrection on the third day, the ascension into heaven, the sitting on the right hand, the coming again a second time in glory,

Choir

Amen

Amen

---

[1] 1 Corr. 11: vv. 23–4; Matt. 26: 26; (John 6: 51).   [2] 1 Cor. 11: 25.   [3] Matt. 26: vv. 27–8; Mark 14: 24; Luke 22: 20.

Thine own, of thine own,[1] we offer unto thee in all and for all,

Here the Deacon crossing his hands shall lift up the holy paten and the holy chalice, bowing himself humbly.

And the Priest continues

Moreover we offer unto thee this reasonable[2] and bloodless service; and we pray, we beseech and implore thee: Send down thy Holy Spirit upon us and upon these gifts here set forth.

Here the Deacon laying down the fan shall approach the Priest, and Priest and Deacon shall incline themselves thrice before the holy altar, praying secretly.

Now the Deacon bowing his head and pointing with his orarion *to the holy bread shall say softly*

| Bless, Master, the holy bread.

And the Priest rising shall make the sign of the cross over the holy bread, saying

And make this bread the precious body of thy Christ.

Deacon

| Amen.

Choir

We hymn thee, we bless thee, we give thanks unto thee, O Lord, and we pray unto thee, our God

---

[1] 1 Chron. 29: 14.   [2] Rom. 12: 1.

	Choir
And the Deacon again | **Bless, Master, the sacred cup.** *And the Priest shall bless it and say* | **And that which is in this cup the precious blood of thy Christ.** *Deacon* | **Amen.** *And pointing to both paten and chalice the Deacon shall say again* | **Master, bless both.** *And the Priest shall bless both saying* | **Transmaking them by thy Holy Spirit.** *Deacon* | **Amen. Amen. Amen.** *And the Deacon bowing his head to the Priest saith* | **Remember me, a sinner, holy Master.** *Priest* | **The Lord God remember thee in his Kingdom, always, now, and for ever: world without end.** *Deacon* | **Amen.**	

And he goes to stand where he was before, and taking the fan he fans the holy things as before, the while the Priest prays

That they may be to them that partake thereof unto vigilance of soul, the remission of sins, the communion of thy Holy Ghost,[1] the fulfilment of the Kingdom of heaven; and for boldness to approach thee, neither unto judgment nor unto condemnation.[2]

Moreover we offer unto thee this reasonable service[3] for them that have gone to their rest in faith: For our forefathers, fathers, patriarchs, prophets, apostles, preachers, evangelists, martyrs, confessors, ascetics; and for every righteous spirit in faith made perfect.[4]

And taking the censer the Priest shall say aloud

More especially our most holy and undefiled, most blessed and glorious Lady, Mother of God and ever-Virgin Mary.

And he shall offer incense three times before the sacred altar.

Meet is it in very truth to call thee blessed who didst bring forth God, ever blessed and most pure, and Mother of our God.

---

[1] 2 Cor. 13: 14.   [2] 1 Cor. 11: 34.   [3] Rom. 12: 1.   [4] Jas. 2: 22.

Then shall the Deacon cense the sacred altar round about, calling to mind as he will the departed and the living.

Choir

More honourable than the cherubim and past compare more glorious than the seraphim, who inviolate didst bear God the Word, very Mother of God, thee we magnify.

The Priest continueth

For S. John, prophet, forerunner and Baptist; For the holy and all glorious apostles; For Saint *N.* whom we call to remembrance this day; And for all thy saints, at whose intercessions visit us, O God.

And do thou remember all them that are fallen asleep in the hope of resurrection unto life eternal.

And he remembers such as he will of the departed, pronouncing their names.

And give them rest where the light of thy countenance[1] watcheth over them.

Also we beseech thee, remember, O Lord, all the Orthodox episcopate who rightly divide the word of thy truth,[2] the whole priesthood, the diaconate which is in Christ, and all clerical and monastic orders.

. Also we offer unto thee this reasonable service[3] for the whole world; for the Holy,

---

[1] Ps. 4: 6.　　[2] 2 Tim. 2: 15.　　[3] Rom. 12: 1.

Catholick and Apostolick Church; for them that live in holiness and honest conversation;[1] for this country and those in authority. And we beseech thee, grant peace to thy world, that we may lead a quiet and peaceable life in all godliness and honesty.[2]

And after the hymn the Priest continueth aloud

And remember first, O Lord, our Patriarch *N.* whom do thou preserve unto thy holy churches that in peace, safety, honour, health and length of days he may rightly divide the word of thy truth.[3]

Remember this city [*or* monastery] in which we live, O Lord, and every city and land, and them that dwell therein with faith. Remember, O Lord, them that travel by land, by water, by air; the sick and the suffering; those in captivity, and their salvation. Remember, O Lord, them that strive[4] and bring forth the fruit of good works in thy holy churches; and them that care for the poor. And upon us all send forth thy mercies.

Choir

And the whole people of God

---

[1] 1 Pet. 2: 12.   [2] 1 Tim. 2: 2.   [3] 2 Tim. 2: 15.   [4] Phil. 1: 27.

And he remembers by name whom he will of the living.

And grant us with one mouth and one heart to glorify[1] and praise thy sublime and wondrous name, of the Father, and of the Son, and of the Holy Ghost; now, and for ever: world without end.

Choir

Amen

And may the mercies of the great God and our Saviour Jesus Christ[2] be with you all.

And with thy spirit

*

THE COMMUNION

Upon a sign of blessing from the Priest, the Deacon goes to stand in the accustomed place saying

Calling to remembrance all the saints, again and again in peace let us pray unto the Lord,

Kyrie eleison

For the precious gifts here offered and hallowed, let us pray unto the Lord,

That our God which loveth mankind; Who hath received them unto his holy and heavenly altar for a sweetsmelling savour[3] of spiritual fragrance may send down upon us divine grace and the gift of the Holy Spirit, let us pray unto the Lord,

That we may be delivered from

---

* *Here shall follow the Ordering of Deacons.*   [1] Rom. 15: 6.   [2] Titus 2: 13.   [3] Eph. 5: 2.

all tribulation, wrath, danger and necessity, let us pray unto the Lord,

Choir

Meanwhile the Priest prays this prayer in secret

> Unto thee we commit our entire being and our confidence, O Sovereign Lord, friend of man; And we pray and beseech thee, and make our supplications: Account us worthy to partake of thy heavenly and dread mysteries at this sacred and spiritual table, with a pure conscience, unto the remission of sins,[1] the forgiveness of transgressions, the communion of the Holy Ghost,[2] an inheritance in the kingdom[3] of heaven, and for boldness to approach thee, neither unto judgment nor unto condemnation.[4]

Deacon

Succour, save, comfort and preserve us, O God, by thy grace,

Kyrie eleison

That this whole day may be perfect, holy, peaceful and without sin, let us entreat the Lord,

Grant us, O Lord

For an angel of peace, faithful guide and guardian of our souls and bodies, let us entreat the Lord,

---

[1] Matt. 26: 28. [2] 2 Cor. 13: 14. [3] Eph. 5: 5. [4] 1 Cor. 11: 34.

For pardon and remission of our sins and transgressions, let us entreat the Lord,

For things good and profitable to our souls, and peace for the world, let us entreat the Lord,

That we may pass the remainder of our lives in peace and repentance, let us entreat the Lord,

For a Christian ending to our life, painless, without shame and peaceful, and a good defence before the dread judgment seat of Christ,[1] let us entreat the Lord,

Having besought the unity of the faith and the communion of the Holy Ghost,[2] let us commend ourselves, and one another, and our whole life to Christ our God,

Choir

To thee, O Lord

Priest

And vouchsafe, O Lord, that boldly and without condemnation we may dare to lift our voices unto thee, O heavenly God and Father, and say

Our Father which art in heaven,
Hallowed be thy Name,
Thy kingdom come,
Thy will be done, in earth as it is in heaven.
Give us this day our daily bread;
And forgive us our trespasses,
As we forgive them that trespass against us;
And lead us not into temptation,
But deliver us from evil.[3]

---

[1] 2 Cor. 5: 10.   [2] 2 Cor. 13: 14.   [3] Matt. 6: vv. 9–13; Luke 11: vv. 2–4; *Book of Common Prayer*.

Priest

For thine is the kingdom, the power and the glory,[1] of the Father, and of the Son, and of the Holy Ghost; now, and for ever: world without end.

Choir

Amen

Priest

Peace unto all.

And unto thy spirit

Deacon

Bow down your heads before the Lord.

To thee, O Lord

Priest

We give thanks unto thee, O King invisible,[2] who by thy measureless power didst fashion all things, and in the multitude of thy mercies[3] didst from non-being bring all things into being. Do thou, O Sovereign Lord, look down from heaven upon them that now bow their heads unto thee; For they are bowed not before flesh and blood but unto thee, O dread God. Bestow on us therefore, O Lord, these thy gifts, giving to each according to his need: Sail with them that sail upon the seas; journey with them that travel on dry land; heal the sick, O thou which art the physician of our souls and bodies,

---

[1] Matt. 6: vv. 9–13; Luke 11: vv. 2–4; *Book of Common Prayer*. [2] 1 Tim. 1: 17. [3] Ps. 51: 1.

Through the bountiful grace and love toward mankind of thine only-begotten Son, with whom thou art blessed together with thy most holy, good and life-giving Spirit; now, and for ever: world without end.

Choir

Amen

The Priest prayeth in a low voice

Give heed,[1] O Lord Jesus Christ, our God, from thy holy dwelling place,[2] and from the glorious throne of thy kingdom;[3] and come to sanctify us,[4] O thou that sittest on high with the Father and art here invisibly present with us. And vouchsafe by thy mighty hand[5] to impart unto us of thy most pure body and precious blood; And through us unto all thy people.

The while the Priest is praying this prayer the Deacon standing before the Holy Doors shall gird his orarion *about him crosswise. Then the Priest and the Deacon likewise in the place where he stands, bowing themselves shall repeat secretly, thrice*

O God, cleanse thou me a sinner, and be merciful to me.[6]

---

[1] Jer. 18: 19.   [2] 2 Chron. 30: 27; 1 Kings 8: 39.   [3] Song of the 3 Childr. v. 33.   [4] 1 Thess. 5: 23.
[5] Deut. 9: 26.   [6] Luke 18: 13.

And when the Deacon seeth the Priest stretch forth his hands and touch the holy bread, to make the elevation, he shall say

Let us give heed.

And the Priest as he lifts up the holy bread shall say

The holy things[1] unto the holy.

Choir

One only is holy,[2] One only is the Lord,[3] Jesus Christ, to the glory of God the Father.[4] Amen

Now the Choir shall chant the anthem for the day [or of the Saint] the while the Deacon shall enter the sanctuary, and standing at the right hand of the Priest shall say

Break, O Master, the holy bread.

And the Priest breaking it in four parts with all heedfulness and awe, shall say

Broken and divided is the Lamb of God; Which being broken yet is not divided; Being ever eaten, never is consumed; But sanctifieth them that partake thereof.

---

[1] Ezek. 22: 26.   [2] Rev. 15: 4.   [3] Eph. 4: 5.   [4] Phil. 2: 11.

Of the Fraction of the holy bread

Know, O priest, when thou dost divide the Holy Lamb, to lay the parts on the holy paten with the sign of the cross downward and the incision upward, as before when it was slain [q.v. page 24]. Lay then IC at the top of the holy paten, which is toward the east, and XC at the bottom, which is toward the west; and NI on the north side, and KA on the south side, as is here figured.

Take then the part IC and fill the holy chalice. But XC divide for the priests and the deacons. The two other portions, namely, the NI and the KA, thou shalt divide into small pieces, as many as are sufficient for the communicants, accordingly to thy discretion. And from the portion which representeth the Holy Mother of God, or from the particles representing the nine ranks of the saints, or others that lie on the holy paten none shall communicate: but only from the two of the Holy Lamb which remain shall the Priest give communion. And here be it known to thee also concerning this, that when thou dost dilute the divine blood of the Lord with the holy zeon, then thou pourest with all care so much as is necessary for all to communicate. After the same manner also of the wine and the water, when thou piercest the Holy Lamb, then pour in so much as is sufficient for all. But afterward in no wise pour in anything but only once at **The holy things unto the Holy.** *And so communicate all with these.*

Then the Deacon pointing with his orarion to the holy chalice shall exclaim

| **Fill, Master, the holy cup.**

And the Priest taking from the paten the particle which lies uppermost, that marked IC, shall make therewith the sign of the cross over the chalice, saying

| **The fulness of the Holy Spirit.**

And thereupon let fall the particle into the cup.

Deacon

| **Amen.**

And taking the warm water he shall say to the Priest

| **Bless, Master, the fervency.**

And the Priest shall perform the bene-diction saying

| **Blessed is the fervency of thy saints; always, now, and for ever: world without end. Amen.**

And the Deacon shall pour into the holy chalice, crosswise, so much as suffices saying

| **The fervency of faith, full of the Holy Spirit. Amen.**

Then setting aside the warm water he shall stand somewhat apart.

And the Priest shall say

| **Deacon, draw near.**

Choir

And the Deacon shall approach and shall make a devout reverence, entreating forgiveness. The Priest then holding the holy bread shall impart it to the Deacon, who shall kiss the Priest's hand and receive the holy bread saying

Impart unto me, O Master, the precious and holy body of our Lord and God and Saviour Jesus Christ.

And the Priest shall say

Unto *N.*, deacon in Holy Orders, is imparted the precious and holy and all pure body of our Lord and God and Saviour Jesus Christ, for the remission of his sins[1] and unto life everlasting.

And the Deacon shall withdraw behind the holy table and bowing his head he shall pray, as doth the Priest

I believe, O Lord . . . [*and the rest, as below*]

The Priest likewise taking a particle of the holy bread shall say

The precious and most holy body of our Lord and God and Saviour Jesus Christ is imparted unto me, *N.*, priest, for the remission of my sins[1] and unto life everlasting.

Choir

---

[1] Matt. 26: 28.

And bowing his head he shall pray saying

| *Choir* |

I believe, O Lord, and confess that thou art in truth the Christ, the Son of the living God,[1] come into the world to save sinners; of whom I am chief.[2] And I believe that this is indeed thine incorruptible body, and this thy most precious blood. Wherefore I pray thee, have mercy upon me, and forgive me my trespasses, voluntary and involuntary, whether of word or deed, witting or unwitting; And vouchsafe that I may partake without condemnation of thy most pure mysteries, for the remission of sins[3] and unto life everlasting. Amen.

Of thy mystical supper, O Son of God, accept me this day as a partaker; For I will not speak of the mystery to thine enemies, nor will I give thee a kiss like Judas;[4] but like the thief I will acknowledge thee: Remember me, O Lord, in thy Kingdom.[5]

And let not this participation in thy holy mysteries be to my judgment nor to my condemnation,[6] O Lord, but unto the healing of soul and body.

---

[1] Matt. 16: 16.   [2] 1 Tim. 1: 15.   [3] Matt. 26: 28.   [4] Matt. 26: 49; Mark 14: 45.
[5] Luke 23: 42.   [6] 1 Cor. 11: 34.

Thus in fear and with all precaution they shall partake of that which they hold in their hands.

Then the Priest drawing himself up shall take the chalice with the veil in both hands and partake of it three times saying

> **Of the precious and holy blood of our Lord and God and Saviour Jesus Christ I the servant of God, *N.*, priest, do partake for the remission of my sins[1] and unto life everlasting. Amen.**

Then wiping his lips and the rim of the chalice with the veil in his hand he shall say

> **Lo, this hath touched my lips; and mine iniquity is taken away, and my sin purged.[2]**

Then he shall summon the Deacon saying

> **Deacon, draw near.**

And the Deacon shall approach and shall make one reverence saying

> **Lo, I draw near unto our immortal King and God. Impart unto me, O Master, the precious and holy blood of our Lord and God and Saviour Jesus Christ.**

Choir

---

[1] Matt. 26: 28.   [2] Isa. 6: 7.

And the Priest shall say

The servant of God, Deacon N., partaketh of the precious and holy blood of our Lord and God and Saviour Jesus Christ for the remission of his sins[1] and unto life everlasting.

When the Deacon has partaken the Priest shall say

Lo, this hath touched thy lips; and thine iniquity is taken away, and thy sin purged.[2]

If there be any that desire to partake of the holy mysteries the Priest shall divide the two remaining portions, the NI and the KA, into small particles, sufficient for all, and place them in the chalice.

And he shall cover the chalice with the veil, and likewise lay the star and the veils over the paten, thereafter saying secretly

We give thee thanks,[3] O Lord, friend of man, who art the benefactor of our souls, for that thou hast accounted us this day to be worthy of thy heavenly and immortal mysteries. Make straight our ways;[4] Stablish us all in thy fear; Watch over our life; Make sure our steps: By the prayers

Choir

---

[1] Matt. 26: 28.　　[2] Isa. 6: 7.　　[3] Rev. 11: 17.　　[4] Matt. 3: 3; Prov. 3: 6.

and supplications of the glorious Mother of God and ever-Virgin Mary, and of all thy saints.

Choir

And thereupon the sanctuary doors are opened. And the Deacon bowing himself low and devoutly taking up the chalice shall approach the Doors and there lifting up the chalice shew it to the people saying

In fear of God and with faith draw near.

Blessed is he that cometh in the name of the Lord: God is the Lord,[1] and hath revealed himself[2] to us.

They that are desirous to communicate shall now approach. And they shall come one by one, bearing themselves with all godly humility and awe, their hands crossed upon their breasts: And in this manner each shall receive the divine mysteries, after the Priest hath said aloud

I believe, O Lord . . . [*and the rest, as above*]

The Priest as he gives communion to each one shall say

The servant of God ∗ ∗ ∗ partaketh of the precious and holy body and blood of our Lord and God and Saviour Jesus Christ, for the remission of his/her sins and unto life everlasting.

---

[1] Ps. 118: vv. 26–7; Matt. 21: 9; Mark 11: 9; Luke 13: 35.   [2] 1 Sam. 3: 21.

As each partakes the Deacon shall wipe their lips with the veil, and the communicant shall kiss the holy chalice, incline his head and go aside [where he is given blessed bread to eat and warm wine with water to drink].

And the Choir sings

When all are houselled the Choir shall sing
And the Priest goeth into the sanctuary and setteth down the holy things upon the holy table.

Then the Deacon holding the paten over the chalice shall say these Hymns of the Resurrection secretly

We have seen the resurrection of Christ, wherefore let us worship the Lord Jesus for that he is holy, he only is without sin. Thy cross, O Christ, we worship, and thy holy resurrection we laud and glorify. For thou art our God, we know none other beside thee, we call upon thy name. O come, all ye faithful, let us bow down and worship Christ's holy resurrection. For behold, by the cross is joy come in all the world. Evermore blessing the Lord, let us sing his resurrection: for in that he endured the cross, death by death hath he destroyed.

Shine, shine, O new Jerusalem, for the glory of the Lord is

Choir

Receive ye the body of Christ
Taste ye of the fountain of life

Alleluia. Alleluia. Alleluia.

risen upon thee.[1] Rejoice now and be glad, O Zion. And do thou rejoice, O pure Mother of God, for the fruit of thy womb is risen again.

O Christ, O great and most sacred Passover![2] O Wisdom and Word of God and Power![3] Grant that we may more truly have communion with thee in the day of thy Kingdom which knoweth no eventide.

With all care and reverence wiping the paten throughly with the holy spunge the Deacon shall say

Wash away, O Lord, the sins of them that have been remembered here, by thy precious blood, at the prayers of thy saints.

The Priest shall then bless the people saying

O God, save thy people, and bless thine inheritance.[4]

And turning to the holy table he shall cense it thrice, saying secretly

Be thou exalted, O God, above the heavens; let thy glory be above all the earth.[5]

Choir

---

[1] Isa. 60: 1.   [2] 1 Cor. 5: 7.   [3] 1 Cor. 1: 24; Rev. 19: 13.   [4] Ps. 28: 9.
[5] Ps. 57: vv. 5, 11.

While the Choir shall sing

Choir

We have seen the true Light; We have received the heavenly Spirit; We have found the true faith. We worship the undivided Trinity: for the same hath saved us.

The Priest then taking the holy paten shall set it upon the head of the Deacon; and the Deacon bearing it with veneration and looking toward the Holy Doors, nothing saying, shall proceed to the offertory-table where he shall set it down.

The Priest meanwhile making a reverence shall take up the holy chalice and turning to face the Holy Doors, and looking to the people, shall say in secret

| Blessed is our God;

And aloud

Always, now, and for ever: world without end.

Amen

And he shall proceed to the offertory-table and there set down the holy things.

And the Choir

Let our mouth be filled with thy praise,[1] O Lord, that we may sing of thy glory: for that thou hast accounted us worthy to partake of thy holy, divine, immortal and life-giving mysteries. Preserve us[2] in thy holiness that we may

---

[1] Ps. 71: 8. [2] Ps. 40: 11.

Choir

think on[1] thy righteousness all the day[2] long.

Alleluia. Alleluia. Alleluia.

And the Deacon going out by the north door and standing in the accustomed place shall say

Be upright. Having partaken of the divine, holy, undefiled, immortal, heavenly, life-giving and fearful mysteries of Christ, let us give rightful thanks unto the Lord,

Kyrie eleison

Succour, save, comfort and preserve us, O God, by thy grace,

Having prayed that this whole day be perfect, holy, peaceful and without sin, let us commend ourselves, and one another, and our whole life to Christ our God,

To thee, O Lord

And the Priest folds up the antiminsion *and holding forth the Book of the Holy Gospels makes a cross over it saying*

For thou art our sanctification,[3] and unto thee we ascribe glory, unto the Father, and unto the Son, and unto the Holy Ghost; now, and for ever: world without end.

Amen

---

[1] Phil. 4: 8.   [2] Ps. 71: 8.   [3] 1 Cor. 1: 30.

THE DISMISSAL

Priest

Let us depart in peace,

Deacon

Let us pray unto the Lord,

Priest
standing below the chancel steps

O Lord who dost bless them that bless thee,[1] **and hallowest them that put their trust in thee: Save thy people, and bless thine inheritance.**[2] **Preserve the fulness of thy Church, and sanctify them that love the beauty of thy house.**[3] **Do thou by thy divine power glorify them, and forsake us not who put our trust in thee. Grant peace to thy world; to thy churches; to thy priests; to those in authority; and to all thy people.**

For every good gift and every perfect gift is from above, and cometh down from thee, the Father of lights:[4] **And to thee we ascribe glory and thanksgiving and worship, to the Father, and to the Son, and to the Holy Ghost; now, and for ever: world without end.**

Choir

In the name of the Lord

Kyrie eleison

Amen

Blessed be the name of the Lord from this time forth and for evermore[5] **[*thrice*]**

---

[1] Num. 24: 9.   [2] Ps. 28: 9.   [3] Ps. 25: 8 (*Septuagint*).   [4] Jas. 1: 17.   [5] Ps. 113: 2.

The Reader shall now read Psalm 34[1]

I will bless the Lord at all times:

During the prayer below the chancel steps the Deacon shall stand on the right side before the ikon of our Lord Christ, holding his orarion *in his hand and bowing his head until the conclusion of the prayer. And when this hath been said the Priest shall enter through the Holy Doors and going to the offertory-table he shall say secretly this prayer the while the remainder of the holy things are being consumed*

> **Forasmuch as thou art thyself the fulfilling of the law[2] and the prophets, O Christ our God, who didst accomplish all things appointed of the Father: Fill our hearts with joy and gladness, always, now, and for ever: world without end.**

The while the Deacon going in by the north side shall consume the holy gifts with all reverence and care, the Priest shall come forth to distribute the anti-doron *to the people. When the Psalm is ended he shall say*

The blessing of the Lord be upon you, by his divine grace and loving-kindness, always, now, and for ever: world without end.

Choir

Amen

---

[1] See p. 205.   [2] Rom. 13: 10.

Glory be unto thee, O Christ our God and our hope,[1] glory be unto thee.

And a Dismissal is made

May Christ our true God [who is risen from the dead], by the prayers of his most holy Mother; by the power of the precious and life-giving cross; by the protection of the heavenly bodiless hosts; through the supplications of the glorious prophet and forerunner, John the Baptist; of the holy and all glorious apostles; of our sacred fathers among the saints, the great hierarchs; of the holy, glorious and triumphant martyrs; of our sacred fathers whom God inspired; of the holy and righteous progenitors of God, Joachim and Anna; of our father among the saints, John Chrysostom, archbishop of Constantinople; of N. [*the saint to whom the church is dedicated*]; of N. to whose memory we dedicate this day; and of all the saints, have mercy upon us, and save our souls: For he is good and loving-kind.

Choir

Glory be unto the Father, and unto the Son, and unto the Holy Ghost; now, and for ever: world without end. Amen

Kyrie eleison [*thrice*]

Master, give the blessing

Amen

---

[1] 1 Tim. 1: 1.

	Choir
The Priest then goeth into the sanctuary and saith the Prayers of Thanksgiving.[1] *After which he shall recite the Song of Simeon,*[2] *the* Trisagion, *and the rest, and the Lord's Prayer. And thereupon the Dismissal* troparion	

Grace shone forth from thy lips like a flame of fire to illumine the universe. Thou didst teach us to neglect the treasures of this world. Thou hast shewn unto us the height of divine humility. Thou whose words are for our admonition,[3] O Father John Chrysostom, pray unto Christ the Word that our souls be saved.

Glory be to the Father, and to the Son, and to the Holy Ghost;

And the kontakion

From on high didst thou receive grace divine, and the words of thy lips instruct all men to worship one God in the Holy Trinity. O blessed Saint John Chrysostom, we rightly praise thee, for thou art our guide who dost manifest things divine.

Now, and for ever: world without end. Amen.

---

[1] See page 211.   [2] *Nunc Dimittis*, Luke 2: vv. 29-32.   [3] 1 Cor. 10: 11.

And the Hymn to the Mother of God

O steadfast help and shield[1] of Christians; Constant advocate with the Creator: Despise not the prayer[2] of sinners who intreat thee; But of thy goodness be swift to succour us that call upon thee in faith. Make speed to pray. Make haste to intercede for us, O Mother of God who dost ever watch over them that honour thee.

[Or such other hymn of the day as may be desired]

Lord, have mercy.   *[12 times]*

More honourable than the cherubim, and past compare more glorious than the seraphim, Who inviolate didst bear God the Word, very Mother of God, thee we magnify.

Glory be to the Father, and to the Son, and to the Holy Ghost; now, and for ever: world without end. Amen.

And he pronounces the Dismissal and puts off his sacred vestments.

The Deacon recites the Song of Simeon and the rest, in like manner with the Priest, first having consumed the holy things with all wariness that no

Choir

---

[1] Ps. 115: 9.   [2] Ps. 102: 17.

smallest particle fall or remain, pouring into the chalice wine and water and consuming it, and wiping the chalice round about with the spunge, and thereafter setting the sacred vessels together, wrapping them and laying them by in the customary place.

The Priest and the Deacon wash their hands at the appointed place; and having done reverence together the Priest shall pronounce the Dismissal. And giving thanks unto God for all things they go their way.

Choir

HERE ENDETH THE DIVINE LITURGY OF S. JOHN CHRYSOSTOM

THE
DIVINE LITURGY
OF OUR FATHER AMONG THE SAINTS
BASIL THE GREAT

From **THE** *ENARXIS* (*page 35*) *to the demand* Ye catechumens, bow your heads unto the Lord (*page 54*) *the Liturgies of S. John Chrysostom and S. Basil the Great are identical. But now the Liturgy of S. Basil continues as follows:*

The Priest shall say	*Choir*

The Prayer for the Catechumens

O Lord our God that dwellest in the heavens,[1] and dost behold all thy works: Look down upon thy servants the catechumens, who have bowed their heads before thee, and give them thine easy yoke.[2] Make them upright members of thy holy Church; and deem them worthy of the washing of regeneration,[3] of the remission of sins,[4] and the garment of incorruption, unto knowledge of thee, our true God,

That they also with us may glorify thy sublime and wondrous name, of the Father, and of the Son, and of the Holy Ghost; now, and for ever: world without end.

Amen

The Priest unfolds the antiminsion.

---

[1] Ps. 123: 1.   [2] Matt. 11: 30.   [3] Titus 3: 5.   [4] Matt. 26: 28.

Deacon	*Choir*
All ye that are catechumens, depart.	
If there be a second Deacon he also shall cry aloud	
Catechumens, depart.	
Then again the first Deacon	
All ye catechumens, depart.	
Let not any of the catechumens remain. All we the faithful, again and again in peace let us pray unto the Lord,	*Kyrie eleison*
If there be but one Deacon he, or if there be no Deacon, the Priest shall say	
All ye that are catechumens, depart. Catechumens, depart. All ye catechumens, depart. Let not any of the catechumens remain. All we the faithful, again and again in peace let us pray unto the Lord,	*Kyrie eleison*

THE LITURGY OF THE FAITHFUL

THE PRAYERS OF THE FAITHFUL

Priest

The First Prayer of the Faithful

Thou, O Lord, hast made known unto us this great mystery[1] of salvation: Thou hast

---

[1] 1 Tim. 3: 16.

counted us,[1] thine humble and unmeritable servants, worthy to be ministers[2] of thy sacred altar. Do thou, through the power of the Holy Ghost,[3] make us able for this ministry,[4] that standing without condemnation before the presence of thy glory[5] we may offer unto thee the sacrifice of praise;[6] For thou it is which workest all in all.[7] Grant, O Lord, that this our sacrifice may be acceptable[8] unto thee, both for our sins and for the errors of the people,[9] and wellpleasing to thee.[10]

Choir

Deacon

Succour, save, comfort and preserve us, O God, by thy grace, Wisdom.

Kyrie eleison

Priest

For unto thee belong all glory, honour and worship, unto the Father, and unto the Son, and unto the Holy Ghost; now, and for ever: world without end.

Amen

Deacon

Again and again in peace let us pray unto the Lord,

Kyrie eleison

---

[1] 1 Tim. 1: 12. [2] 2 Cor. 3: 6. [3] Rom. 15: 13. [4] 2 Cor. 4: 1. [5] Jude v. 24; Song of the 3 Childr. v. 31. [6] Heb. 13: 15. [7] 1 Cor. 12: 6. [8] Rom. 15: 16; 1 Pet. 2: 5. [9] Heb. 9: 7. [10] Phil. 4: 18.

[When the Priest celebrates without a deacon he omits the petitions here following]

For the peace from on high, and for the salvation of our souls, let us pray unto the Lord,

For the peace and union of the whole world, and for the good estate of the holy churches of God, let us pray unto the Lord,

For this holy temple and for them that enter therein with faith, reverence and fear of God, let us pray unto the Lord,

That we may be delivered from all tribulation, wrath, danger and necessity, let us pray unto the Lord,

After which the Priest shall pray

The Second Prayer of the Faithful

O God who with loving-kindness and tender mercies[1] hast visited our lowly estate; Who hast set us, thine humble, sinful and unworthy servants, before thine holy glory[2] to minister at thy sacred altar: Do thou through the power of the Holy Ghost[3] strengthen us for this ministry, and give us utterance that our mouths may be opened[4] to invoke the grace of thy Holy Spirit upon the gifts that we would lay before thee.

Choir

---

[1] Ps. 103: 4.   [2] Jude v. 24; Song of the 3 Childr. v. 31.   [3] Rom. 15: 13.   [4] Eph. 6: 19.

Deacon	*Choir*
Succour, save, comfort and pre-serve us, O God, by thy grace, Wisdom.	***Kyrie eleison***
Priest	
That being ever guarded by thy might we may give glory to thee, to the Father, and to the Son, and to the Holy Ghost; now, and for ever: world without end.	Amen

THE OFFERTORY

Here Priest and Deacon continue as in the Liturgy of S. John Chrysostom, the Priest praying silently within himself

None is worthy among them that are held fast in fleshly desires and pleasures to approach thee, or draw nigh and minister unto thee, O King of glory.[1] For to minister unto thee is a great and fearful thing, even for the heavenly powers themselves. Yet do we presume to serve thee forasmuch as in thine ineffable and immeasurable love toward mankind thou didst become Man, suffering thereby no change or altering, and art thyself made an high priest for us, and thyself didst bestow upon us the working of this

Let us the cherubim mystically representing, and unto the life-giving Trinity the thrice-holy chant intoning, now lay aside all earthly care.

---

[1] Ps. 24: vv. 7-10.

divine office, of this bloodless sacrifice, as Master of all: For thou only, O Lord our God, hast dominion over heaven and earth, who art borne by the cherubim upon the throne, who art Lord of the seraphim and King of Israel;[1] Who only art holy and dost rest in the holies.[2]

Wherefore I make my supplication unto thee who alone art good and ready to hear. Look down upon me, thy sinful and unprofitable servant,[3] and cleanse my soul and my heart from an evil conscience.[4] And by the power of thy Holy Spirit enable me, who am invested with the grace of priesthood, to stand before this thy holy table, and to administer thy most pure and sacred body and thy precious blood. For unto thee I come, to thee I bow my head, and I beseech thee: Turn not thy face from me, neither reject me from among thy servants; but account it meet that these gifts be offered unto thee by me, thy sinful and unworthy servant. For thou art both he that offereth and he that is offered. Thou dost receive and art given, O Christ

Choir

---

[1] John 1: 49.   [2] Isa. 57: 15 (*Septuagint*).   [3] Luke 17: 10.   [4] Heb. 10: 22.

our God, and unto thee we ascribe glory, together with thine eternal Father, and thy most holy, gracious and life-giving Spirit; now, and for ever: world without end. Amen.

The prayer and the censing alike being finished, the Priest and the Deacon standing before the holy table them-selves rehearse the Cherubic Hymn three times, making a reverence at the end of each repetition.

Priest

Let us the cherubim mystically representing, and unto the life-giving Trinity the thrice-holy chant intoning, now lay aside all earthly care:

Deacon

That we may raise on high the King of all, by the angelic hosts invisibly attended.

Alleluia. Alleluia. Alleluia.

But on Thursday in Holy Week this only shall be sung

Choir

Of thy mystical supper, O Son of God, accept me this day as a partaker; For I will not speak of the mystery to thine enemies, nor will I give thee a kiss like Judas;[1] but like the thief I will acknow-ledge thee: Remember me, O Lord, in thy Kingdom.[2]

Alleluia. Alleluia. Alleluia.

---

[1] Matt. 26: 49; Mark 14: 45.   [2] Luke 23: 42.

And on Saturday in Holy Week this is to be sung

Choir

Let all mortal flesh be still, and stand with fearfulness and trembling,[1] minding not earthly things,[2] for the King of kings and Lord of lords[3] cometh to be slain[4] and to give himself for food[5] to the faithful. Behold, before him go the angelic hosts with all the principalities and powers,[6] the many-eyed cherubim and the six-winged seraphim[7] covering their faces and crying aloud:

Alleluia. Alleluia. Alleluia.

Then shall they proceed to the offertory-table, the Deacon going first, and the Priest shall cense the holy gifts, praying secretly the while

| O God, cleanse thou me, a sinner.

The Deacon saith unto the Priest

| Take, Master.

And the Priest taking the aer *shall lay it on the Deacon's left shoulder and shall say*

| Lift up your hands in the sanctuary, and bless the Lord.[8]

Then taking the paten he shall set it on the Deacon's head with all care and reverence, the Deacon the while holding

---

[1] Ps. 55: 5.   [2] Phil. 3: 19.   [3] 1 Tim. 6: 15.   [4] Luke 9: 22.   [5] Ps. 136: 25.
[6] Eph. 3: 10.   [7] Isa. 6: vv. 2–3.   [8] Ps. 134: 2.

the censer with one finger of his right hand. The chalice the Priest shall himself take in his hands, and both shall go forth at the north side, preceded by lighted tapers.

And they shall go round about the nave, each praying in turn for such as he will, at his discretion, and finally the Priest shall say

May the Lord God remember in his Kingdom you, and all faithful Christians; always, now, and for ever: world without end.

The Deacon going in at the Holy Doors stands to the right and as the Priest enters he shall say to him

May the Lord God remember thy priesthood in his Kingdom.

And the Priest to him

May the Lord God remember thy sacred ministry in his Kingdom: always, now, and for ever: world without end.

And the Priest shall then set the holy chalice upon the altar, and taking from the Deacon's head the holy paten he sets it down likewise, saying

Down from the tree Joseph, a godly man, took thy most pure body, and wound it in linen clothes with the spices, and

Choir

Amen

That we may raise on high the King of all, by the angelic hosts invisibly attended.

Alleluia. Alleluia. Alleluia.

laid and closed it in a new sepulchre.[1]

In the tomb according to the flesh,
As God in hell with the soul,
In paradise with the thief,
And on the throne with the Father and the Spirit
Wast thou, O Christ, omni-present, incircumscript.

Thy life-giving tomb is revealed to us
Lovelier far than paradise,
More radiant than a king's palace,
O Christ, the well-spring of our resurrection.

Then shall he take the veils from the paten and the chalice, and shall lay them on one side of the holy altar; and taking the aer *from the Deacon's shoulder and censing it he shall cover therewith the holy gifts, and shall say*

Down from the tree Joseph, a godly man, took thy most pure body, and wound it in linen clothes with the spices, and laid and closed it in a new sepulchre.[1]

And taking the censer from the hands of the Deacon he shall cense the holy gifts three times, saying the while

Do good in thy good pleasure

Choir

---

[1] John 19: vv. 40-1.

unto Zion: build thou the walls of Jerusalem.

Then shalt thou be pleased with the sacrifices of right-eousness, with burnt offering and whole burnt offering: then shall they offer bullocks upon thine altar.[1]

And giving back the censer he shall bow his head and say to the Deacon

Remember me, brother and fellow-minister.

And the Deacon shall say to him

May the Lord God remember thy priesthood in his King-dom.

And the Deacon likewise bowing his head and holding his orarion *the while with three fingers of his right hand shall say to the Priest*

| Pray for me, reverend Master.

Priest

The Holy Ghost shall come upon thee, and the power of the Highest shall overshadow thee.[2]

Deacon

The same Spirit shall labour with us all the days of our life.

Choir

---

[1] Ps 51: vv. 18-19   [2] Luke 1: 35.

And the Deacon again

| Remember me, reverend Master.

Priest

| The Lord God remember thee in his Kingdom; always, now, and for ever: world without end.

Deacon

| Amen.

*

And having kissed the Priest's right hand he goes out at the north door and standing in his customary place he shall say

Let us complete our supplication unto the Lord,

   For the precious gifts here set forth, let us pray unto the Lord,

   For this holy temple and for them that enter therein with faith, reverence and fear of God, let us pray unto the Lord,

   That we may be delivered from all tribulation, wrath, danger and necessity, let us pray unto the Lord,

After he has set the divine gifts upon the holy altar the Priest shall pronounce

Choir

Kyrie eleison

---

* *Here shall follow the Ordering of a Priest.*

The Offertory Prayer

O Lord our God who hast created us and brought us into this life; Who hast shewn unto us the way of salvation;[1] Who hast given us the revelation of heavenly mysteries: For that thou hast appointed us unto this ministry, by the power of thy Holy Spirit, suffer us, O Lord, to be ministers of thy new testament,[2] and servants of thy holy sacraments. According to the greatness of thy mercy[3] do thou accept us who now draw nigh unto thy sacred altar, that we may be worthy to offer unto thee this reasonable and bloodless sacrifice for our sins and for the errors of the people:[4] and receiving the same for a sweetsmelling savour[5] unto thy holy altar far above all heavens,[6] send down upon us the grace of thy Holy Spirit. Look upon us, O God, and behold this our service, which do thou accept even as thou didst accept the offering of Abel,[7] the burnt offerings of Noah,[8] the whole burnt offering of Abraham,[9] the sacred offerings of Moses and Aaron, the peace offerings of Samuel.[10] Even as thou didst receive from

Choir

---

[1] Acts 16: 17.   [2] 2 Cor. 3: 6.   [3] Neh. 13: 22.   [4] Heb. 9: 7.   [5] Eph. 5: 2.
[6] Eph. 4: 10.   [7] Gen. 4: 4.   [8] Gen. 8: 20.   [9] Gen. 22: 13.   [10] 1 Sam. 10: 8.

thy holy apostles this true worship, so also, O Lord, do thou of thy goodness accept these gifts at the hands of us sinners: that counted worthy to serve blamelessly before thy holy altar we may obtain the reward of faithful and wise stewards[1] in the fearful day of thy just recompense.

Choir

Deacon

Succour, save, comfort and preserve us, O God, by thy grace,

Kyrie eleison

That this whole day may be perfect, holy, peaceful and without sin, let us entreat the Lord,

Grant us, O Lord

For an angel of peace, faithful guide and guardian of our souls and bodies, let us entreat the Lord,

For pardon and remission of our sins and transgressions, let us entreat the Lord,

For things good and profitable to our souls, and peace for the world, let us entreat the Lord,

That we may pass the remainder of our lives in peace and repentance, let us entreat the Lord,

For a Christian ending to our life, painless, without shame and peaceful, and a good defence before the dread judgment seat of Christ,[2] let us entreat the Lord,

---

[1] Luke 12: 42.   [2] 2 Cor. 5: 10.

Mindful of our most holy and undefiled, most blessed and glorious Lady, Mother of God and ever-Virgin Mary; and of all the saints; Let us commend ourselves and one another, and our whole life to Christ our God,

Choir

To thee, O Lord

Priest

Through the bountiful mercies of thine only-begotten Son, with whom thou art blessed; together with thy most holy, good and life-giving Spirit; now, and for ever: world without end.

Amen

THE KISS OF PEACE

Priest

Peace unto all.

And unto thy spirit

Deacon

Let us love one another that with one mind we may confess

And the Priest shall bow himself thrice and say secretly within himself

The Father, and the Son, and the Holy Spirit, Trinity consubstantial and undivided

I will love thee, O Lord, my strength.
The Lord is my rock, and my fortress.[1]

And the Deacon shall bow himself thrice and kiss his orarion, *and cry aloud*

The doors, the doors. In wisdom let us give heed.

[1] Ps. 18: vv. 1-2.

THE CREED

Choir

I BELIEVE in one God the Father Almighty, Maker of heaven and earth, And of all things visible and invisible:

And in one Lord Jesus Christ, the only-begotten Son of God, Begotten of the Father before all worlds, Light of Light, Very God of very God, Begotten, not made, Being of one substance with the Father, By whom all things were made: Who for us men and for our salvation came down from heaven, And was incarnate of the Holy Ghost and the Virgin Mary, And was made man, And was crucified also for us under Pontius Pilate. He suffered and was buried, And the third day he rose again according to the Scriptures, And ascended into heaven, And sitteth on the right hand of the Father. And he shall come again with glory to judge both the quick and the dead: Whose kingdom shall have no end.

And in the Holy Ghost, The Lord and giver of life, Who proceedeth from the Father, Who with the Father and the Son together is worshipped and glorified, Who spake by the Prophets.

And in one Holy, Catholick

Choir

and Apostolick Church. I acknowledge one Baptism for the
remission of sins. And I look for
the Resurrection of the dead,
And the life of the world to come.
Amen.

THE *ANAPHORA*

Deacon

Let us be upright, let us stand
with fear, let us take heed to present the holy offering in peace.

The mercy of peace, the sacrifice
of praise

Priest

The grace of our Lord Jesus
Christ, and the love of God the
Father, and the communion of
the Holy Ghost, be with you all.[1]

Let us lift up our hearts.

Let us give thanks unto the
Lord.

And with thy spirit
We lift them up unto the Lord

It is meet and right so to worship
the Father, and the Son, and the
Holy Spirit, Trinity consubstantial and undivided.

*With head bowed the Priest shall now
offer this secret prayer*

O Thou Who Art, O Master
and Lord, God the Father,
Almighty and proper to be
worshipped: It is very meet,
right and befitting the majesty
of thy holiness that we should

---

[1] 2 Cor. 13: 14.

praise thee, and sing unto thee, bless and adore thee, give thanks and glorify thee, of certainty the one true God; that we should bring unto thee this our reasonable service[1] from a contrite heart and an humble spirit.[2] For it is thou who hast vouchsafed unto us the knowledge of thy truth.[3] And who can utter thy mighty acts? Who can shew forth all thy praise, or tell of all thy wondrous works[4] at all times? O sovereign Lord of heaven and earth[5] and of all creation, visible and invisible; Thou that sittest in the throne of glory[6] and dost behold the depths;[7] Who art from everlasting,[8] invisible, searchless, uncircumscribed, immutable,[9] the Father of our Lord Jesus Christ, our great God and Saviour[10] which is our hope,[11] which is the image of thy goodness,[12] equal mould of thy likeness, shewing thee the Father in Himself, the living Word, true God, pre-eternal wisdom, life, sanctification, power,[13] the true light through whom was manifest the Holy Spirit: the Spirit of truth,[14] the grace of the adoption of sons,[15]

Choir

---

[1] Rom. 12: 1.   [2] Song of the 3 Childr. v. 16.   [3] Heb. 10: 26.   [4] Ps. 105: 2.
[5] Matt. 11: 25.   [6] Matt. 19: 28.   [7] Song of the 3 Childr. v. 32.   [8] Ps. 90: 2.
[9] Heb. 6: 18.   [10] Titus. 2: 13.   [11] 1 Tim. 1: 1.   [12] Wisdom of Solomon 7: 26; Col. 1: 15; Heb. 1: 3.   [13] 1 Cor. 1: 24; John 14: 6; 1 Cor. 1: 30.   [14] John 14: 17.   [15] Gal. 4: 5.

the earnest of our inheritance[1] to come, the first-fruits of everlasting good, the quickening power, the fountain of holiness that enableth every creature having reason, and having understanding[2] to serve thee and pour forth an unceasing hymn of glory, for all are thy servants:[3] angels and archangels, thrones, dominions, principalities, powers[4] and virtues, and the many-eyed cherubim[5] praise thee; about thee stand the seraphim, six wings hath the one and six wings hath the other: with twain they cover their faces, and with twain they cover their feet, and with twain they do fly, crying one unto another, with continuing voice unstilled songs of praise,

Singing the triumphal hymn, exclaiming, crying aloud and saying

Choir

Holy, holy, holy, is the Lord of Sabaoth:[6] heaven and earth are full of thy glory. Hosanna in the highest. Blessed is he that cometh in the name of the Lord; Hosanna in the highest.[7]

---

[1] Eph. 1: 14.　　[2] Neh. 10: 28.　　[3] Ps. 119: 91.　　[4] Col. 1: 16.　　[5] Ezek. 1: 18; Rev. 4: 8.　　[6] Rom. 9: 29.　　[7] Isa. 6: vv. 2–3; Matt. 21: 9; Mark 11: vv. 9–10.

	Choir
Here again the Deacon taking the asterisk from off the holy paten shall make the sign of the cross over it and shall kiss it and lay it on one side. He shall then go to stand on the right side of the altar and there taking the fan in his hand shall wave it gently with all care and reverence over the sacred gifts, lest any fly or other insect settle thereon. (If there be no fan he shall use one of the veils.)	

The Priest prayeth

And with these blessed Powers, O sovereign Lord and friend of man, we sinners also cry aloud and say: Holy indeed and most holy art thou, and no bounds are there to the majesty of thy holiness; and just art thou[1] in all thy works, for in righteousness and true judgment hast thou ordered all things for us. For after thou hadst formed man of the dust of the ground,[2] and honoured him, O God, with thine own image,[3] thou didst set him in the garden of Eden, and didst promise unto him immortal life and the joy of everlasting good in the keeping of thy commandments. But man disobeyed thee, his true God which created him, and was allured by the deceit of the serpent, and slain by his

---

[1] Acts 7: 52.   [2] Gen. 2: 7.   [3] Gen. 1: 27.

own trespasses; and thou, O Lord, in righteous judgment didst turn him away from paradise into this world, into the ground from whence he was taken: establishing for him salvation by regeneration, which is in thy Christ himself. For thou, good Master, didst not wholly forsake thy creature which thou hadst made, neither didst thou forget the works of thy hands[1] but because of thy tender mercy in divers manners didst visit him. Prophets didst thou send, mighty works hast thou performed through thy saints which have been wellpleasing unto thee in every generation: thou hast spoken unto us by the mouth of thy servants the prophets, foretelling unto us the salvation to come. Thou gavest the law for an help. Thou didst appoint angels over us to guard us. And when the fulness of the time was come[2] thou didst speak unto us by thy Son himself, by whom also thou madest the worlds. Who, being the brightness of thy glory, and the express image of thy person,[3] and upholding all things by the word of his power, thought it not

Choir

---

[1] Ps. 138: 8.   [2] Gal. 4: 4.   [3] Heb. 1: 3.

robbery to be equal with thee, God[1] and Father. But being God pre-eternal did he yet shew himself upon earth, and conversed with men:[2] and being incarnate of the holy Virgin he emptied himself and took upon him the form of a servant,[3] being made in the likeness of our vile body that he might fashion us like unto the image of his glory:[4] For inasmuch as by one man sin entered into the world, and death by sin,[5] so it seemed good unto thine only-begotten Son, which is in the bosom of thee, O God and Father,[6] made of a woman,[7] the holy Mother of God and ever-Virgin Mary, made under the law,[7] to condemn sin in his flesh,[8] that they who die in Adam may be quickened[9] in thy Christ himself: Who dwelling in this world gave saving commandments and having turned us from the deceits of idols, hath brought us unto knowledge of thee, the true God and Father, having possessed us unto himself for a peculiar people, a royal priesthood, an holy nation:[10] Who hath cleansed us with water and sanctified us[11] by the Holy

Choir

---

[1] Phil. 2: 6.   [2] Baruch 3: 37.   [3] Phil. 2: 7.   [4] Phil. 3: 21; Rom. 8: 29.   [5] Rom. 5: 12.
[6] John 1: 18.   [7] Gal. 4: 4.   [8] Rom. 8: 3.   [9] Eph. 2: 1.   [10] 1 Pet. 2: 9; Titus 2: 14.
[11] Eph. 5: 26.

Ghost,[1] giving himself a ransom unto death, wherein we were held,[2] sold under sin:[3] and by the cross having descended into hell, that he might fill all things with himself,[4] he loosed the pains of death:[5] and being risen again the third day he made a way for all flesh unto the resurrection of the dead, because it was not possible that the author[6] of life should be holden[5] of corruption. So is he become the first-fruits of them that slept,[7] the firstborn from the dead: that in all things he might have the pre-eminence.[8] And ascending into heaven he sat down on the right hand of thy Majesty on high,[9] from whence he shall come again to render to every man according to his deeds.[10] Who also hath left unto us for a remembrance of his saving passion these things which we here set forth according to his commandments. Who being about to go forth to his voluntary and ever-memorable and life-giving death, in the night that he gave himself for the life of the world, took bread in his sacred and most pure hands

Choir

---

[1] Rom. 15: 16.   [2] Rom. 7: 6.   [3] Rom. 7: 14.   [4] Eph. 4: 10.   [5] Acts 2: 24.
[6] Heb. 12: 2.   [7] 1 Cor. 15: 20.   [8] Col. 1: 18.   [9] Heb. 1: 3.   [10] Rom. 2: 6.

and shewing it unto thee, O God and Father, when he had given thanks, and blessed and hallowed it, he brake it

And gave it to his holy disciples and apostles, saying: Take, eat; this is my body which is broken for you[1] for the remission of sins.

The Deacon meanwhile holding his orarion with three fingers of his right hand, shall shew the Priest the paten, and then in like manner the chalice, while the Priest saith

Likewise he took the cup[2] with the fruit of the vine,[3] and when he had mingled it, had given thanks, blessed and hallowed it,

He gave it to his holy disciples and apostles, saying Drink ye all of it; This is my blood of the new testament, which is shed for you and for many for the remission of sins.[4]

And with bowed head the Priest shall continue silently

Do this in remembrance of me: for as often as ye eat this bread, and drink this cup, ye do shew my death[5] and confess my resurrection. Wherefore

Choir

Amen

Amen

---

[1] 1 Cor. 11: vv. 23, 24; Matt. 26: 26; (John 6: 51).   [2] Luke 22: 20; 1 Cor. 11: 25.   [3] Matt. 26: 29.
[4] Matt. 26: vv. 27-8; Mark 14: 24; Luke 22: 20.   [5] 1 Cor. 11: vv. 25-6.

we also, O Master, having in remembrance his redeeming passion and life-giving cross, the three days he was in the tomb, his resurrection from the dead, his ascension into heaven and his sitting on the right hand of thee, God[1] and Father, and his glorious and dread coming again,

Thine own, of thine own,[2] we offer unto thee, in all and for all,

Choir

We hymn thee, we bless thee, we give thanks unto thee, O Lord, and we pray unto thee, our God

With head bowed the Priest prayeth

Wherefore, all holy Lord, we also thy sinful and unworthy servants whom thou hast suffered to minister at thy hallowed altar, not for our righteousnesses[3] for we have done no good thing on earth, but for thy mercy and the bounties which thou hast shed on us abundantly,[4] we presume to draw nigh unto thy holy altar and presenting unto thee the figures[5] of the sacred body and blood of thy Christ, we pray thee and beseech thee, O Holy of Holies, of the good pleasure of thy goodness[6] let thy Holy Ghost come upon us

---

[1] Mark 16: 19; Col. 3: 1.   [2] 1 Chron. 29: 14.   [3] Dan. 9: 18; Titus 3: 5.   [4] Titus 3: 6.
[5] Heb. 9: 24.   [6] 2 Thess. 1: 11.

and upon these gifts here set forth, to bless, hallow and make

Here the Deacon laying down the fan, or the veil, shall approach the Priest, and Priest and Deacon shall incline themselves thrice before the holy altar, praying secretly

| O God, cleanse thou me a sinner, and be merciful to me.[1]

Now the Deacon bowing his head and pointing with his orarion *to the holy bread shall say softly*

| Bless, Master, the holy bread.

Here the Priest signs the bread three times with the sign of the cross saying

| This bread the precious and very body of our Lord and God and Saviour Jesus Christ:

Deacon

| Amen.

And the Deacon again

| Bless, Master, the sacred cup.

The Priest shall bless it and say

| And this cup the precious and very blood of our Lord and God and Saviour Jesus Christ:

Deacon

| Amen.

Choir

---

[1] Luke 18: 13.

Priest	*Choir*
Which was shed for the life of the world,	

Deacon

| **Amen.**

And pointing to both paten and chalice with his orarion *the Deacon shall say again*

| **Master, bless both.**

And the Priest shall bless both saying

| **Transmaking them by thy Holy Spirit.**

Deacon

| **Amen. Amen. Amen.**

And the Deacon bowing his head to the Priest saith

| **Remember me, a sinner, holy Master.**

Priest

| **The Lord God remember thee in his Kingdom, always, now, and for ever: world without end.**

Deacon

| **Amen.**

And he shall go to stand where he was before, the while the Priest prayeth

| **And unite us all one with another, as many as are partakers of the one bread and cup in the communion of the one Holy Spirit. And suffer none to**

partake of the holy body and blood of thy Christ unto judgment or condemnation; But grant that we may obtain mercy and grace,[1] together with all the saints which have been wellpleasing unto thee since the world began; with our forefathers and fathers, patriarchs, prophets, apostles, preachers, evangelists, martyrs, confessors, preceptors: And with every righteous spirit in faith made perfect.[2]

And taking the censer the Priest shall say aloud

More especially our most holy and undefiled, most blessed and glorious Lady, Mother of God and ever-Virgin Mary,

Choir

Hail, thou that art full of grace,
All creatures do rejoice in thee,
The assembly of angels
And all the human race.
O hallowed temple, mystical paradise,
Glory of virgins,
Of whom God, our God before all worlds,
Was incarnate, and was made man.
In thee did He set His throne.
Thou art greater than the heavens.
In thee all creation doth rejoice,
O full of grace, glory to thee.

With S. John, prophet, forerunner and Baptist; the holy and all glorious apostles; Saint *N.* whom we call to remembrance this day; and all thy saints, at whose intercessions visit us, O God.

And do thou remember all them that are fallen asleep in the hope of resurrection unto life eternal, *** *** ***, and give them rest where the light of thy countenance[3] watcheth over them.

---

[1] Heb. 4: 16.   [2] Jas. 2: 22.   [3] Ps. 4: 6.

Also we pray thee remember, O Lord, thy Holy, Catholick and Apostolick Church that stretcheth unto the ends of the earth,[1] and extend thy peace to her[2] which thou hast purchased with the precious blood of thy Christ;[3] And stablish this holy temple even unto the end of the world.[4]

Remember, O Lord, them that have set before thee these gifts; and them for whom and by whom and in behalf of whom they are offered.

Remember, O Lord, them that strive[5] and bring forth the fruit of good works in thy holy churches; and them that care for the poor. Reward them with thy rich and heavenly bounty, for earthly things bestowing on them heavenly things;[6] things eternal for things temporal,[7] things incorruptible for things corruptible.[8]

Remember, O Lord, them that wander in deserts, and in mountains, and in dens and caves of the earth.[9]

Remember, O Lord, them that continue in their virginity, in reverence, in fasting, and in chaste conversation.[10]

Choir

---

[1] Ps. 72: 8.   [2] Isa. 66: 12.   [3] Acts 20: 28; 1 Pet. 1: 19.   [4] Matt. 28: 20.   [5] Phil. 1: 27.
[6] John 3: 12.   [7] 2 Cor. 4: 18.   [8] 1 Cor. 9: 25.   [9] Heb. 11: 38.   [10] 1 Pet. 3: 2.

Remember, O Lord, all that are in authority.[1] Grant them peace, deep and inviolable. Inspire their hearts with good things for thy Church and for all thy people, that in their peace we may lead a quiet and peaceable life in all godliness and honesty.[1] Preserve them that are good in thy goodness; and of thy kindness[2] make them that are evil good. Remember, O Lord, this congregation here present and them that upon their reasonable occasions are absent; and have mercy upon them and upon us, according to the greatness of thy mercy.[3] Fill their store-houses with all manner of good. Maintain their marriage-bonds in peace and concord. Nourish[4] the infants; instruct the young, succour the agèd; comfort the faint-hearted; gather together in one them that are scattered,[5] bring back them which went astray[6] and unite them to thy Holy, Catholick and Apostolick Church. Set free them that are vexed with unclean spirits.[7] Sail with them that sail; journey with them that journey. Defend the widows; shelter the

Choir

---

[1] 1 Tim. 2: 2.   [2] Titus 3: 4.   [3] Neh. 13: 22.   [4] Acts 7: 21.   [5] John 11: 52.
[6] Matt. 18: 13.   [7] Luke 6: 18.

orphans; deliver the captives; heal the sick.

Remember, O God, them that stand trial, that are in prisons, that live in exile; and all that are in affliction and tribulation. Likewise, O God, all them that have need of thy great and tender mercy; them that love us and them that care not for us; and such as have enjoined us, unworthy though we be, to pray for them.

And all thy people remember, O Lord our God; and upon them all pour out thy rich mercy,[1] granting unto all such of their petitions as are unto salvation.

And them that we have not remembered, through ignorance or forgetfulness, or by reason of the multitude of names, do thou thyself call to mind, O God which knowest the days and name of each, and knowest every man from his mother's womb.

For thou, O Lord, art the help of the helpless, the hope of the hopeless, the saviour of them that are storm-tossed, the haven of those in peril, the physician of them that are sick. Be thou thyself all things to all men,[2] which knowest each and

Choir

---

[1] Eph. 2: 4.   [2] 1 Cor. 9: 22.

his petition, his abode and his need.

Preserve this city [or monastery]; and every city and land from famine, pestilences, earthquakes, flood, fire, sword; from the invasion of enemies and from civil strife.

And remember first, O Lord, our Patriarch N. whom do thou preserve unto thy holy churches, that in peace, safety, honour, health and length of days he may rightly divide the word of thy truth.[1]

Remember, O Lord, all the Orthodox episcopate who rightly divide the word of thy truth.[1]

Remember, O Lord, according unto the multitude of thy tender mercies[2] my unworthiness. Forgive me all my trespasses, voluntary and involuntary: and withhold not because of my sins the grace of thy Holy Spirit from the gifts here set forth.

Remember, O Lord, the priesthood, the diaconate which is in Christ, and all clerical and monastic orders; and put none of us to shame who compass thine altar.[3] Visit us, O Lord, of thy clemency.[4]

Choir

And the whole people of God

---

[1] 2 Tim. 2: 15.   [2] Ps. 51: 1.   [3] Ps. 26: 6.   [4] Acts. 24: 4.

Choir

Deal bountifully with us. Vouchsafe unto us temperate winds and fair seasons. Send gentle rains that the land shall yield her increase.[1] Crown the year with thy goodness.[2] Cause divisions to cease in the Churches. Quench the raging of the heathen.[3] By the power of thy Holy Spirit speedily destroy the uprisings of heresy. Receive us all into thy kingdom, having made us children of light, children of the day.[4] Thy peace and thy love grant unto us, O Lord our God, for thou hast rendered to us all things.[5]

And grant us with one mouth and one heart to glorify[6] and praise thy sublime and wondrous name, of the Father, and of the Son, and of the Holy Ghost; now, and for ever: world without end.

Amen

And may the mercies of the great God and our Saviour Jesus Christ[7] be with you all.

And with thy spirit

*

THE COMMUNION

Deacon

Calling to remembrance all the saints, again and again in peace let us pray unto the Lord,

Kyrie eleison

---

[1] Lev. 26: 4.   [2] Ps. 65: 11.   [3] Ps. 2: 1.   [4] 1 Thess. 5: 5.   [5] Isa. 26: 12 (*Septuagint*).
[6] Rom. 15: 6.   [7] Titus 2: 13.   * *Here shall follow the Ordering of Deacons.*

Choir

For the precious gifts here offered and hallowed, let us pray unto the Lord,

That our God which loveth mankind; Who hath received them unto his holy and heavenly altar for a sweetsmelling savour[1] of spiritual fragrance may send down upon us divine grace and the gift of the Holy Spirit, let us pray unto the Lord,

That we may be delivered from all tribulation, wrath, danger and necessity, let us pray unto the Lord,

The Priest prays this prayer silently

Our God, God of salvation, do thou instruct us how we may worthily give thanks unto thee for thy benefits with which thou daily loadest us.[2] Consenting to these gifts do thou, our God, cleanse us from all filthiness of the flesh and spirit; and teach us to perfect holiness in thy fear;[3] that we with the testimony of a pure conscience,[4] receiving a part of thy holy things, may be united with the sacred body and blood of thy Christ; and having received them worthily may have Christ dwelling in our hearts,[5] and may become the temple of thy Holy Ghost.

---

[1] Eph. 5: 2.   [2] Ps. 68: 19.   [3] 2 Cor. 7: 1.   [4] 2 Cor. 1: 12.   [5] Eph. 3: 17.

Yea, O God, let none of us be made guilty by reason of these fearful and heavenly mysteries, or weak in soul or body through an unworthy partaking of the same: But grant us even unto our last breath worthily to receive part of thy hallowed things, unto provision for the way[1] of eternal life and an acceptable defence at the dread judgment seat of thy Christ.[2] That we also with all the saints which have been wellpleasing unto thee since the world began may be made partakers of thine everlasting good things, which thou hast prepared for them that love thee,[3] O Lord.

Deacon

Succour, save, comfort and preserve us, O God, by thy grace,

That this whole day may be perfect, holy, peaceful and without sin, let us entreat the Lord,

For an angel of peace, faithful guide and guardian of our souls and bodies, let us entreat the Lord,

For pardon and remission of our sins and transgressions, let us entreat the Lord,

For things good and profitable

Choir

Kyrie eleison

Grant us, O Lord

---

[1] Gen. 42: 25.   [2] 2 Cor. 5: 10.   [3] 1 Cor. 2: 9.

to our souls, and peace for the world, let us entreat the Lord,

That we may pass the remainder of our lives in peace and repentance, let us entreat the Lord,

For a Christian ending to our life, painless, without shame and peaceful, and a good defence before the dread judgment seat of Christ,[1] let us entreat the Lord,

Having besought the unity of the faith, and the communion of the Holy Ghost,[2] let us commend ourselves, and one another, and our whole life to Christ our God,

Choir

To thee, O Lord

Priest

And vouchsafe, O Lord, that boldly and without condemnation we may dare to lift our voices unto thee, O heavenly God and Father, and say

Our Father which art in heaven,
Hallowed be thy Name,
Thy kingdom come,
Thy will be done, in earth as it is in heaven.
Give us this day our daily bread;
And forgive us our trespasses,
As we forgive them that trespass against us;
And lead us not into temptation,
But deliver us from evil.[3]

---

[1] 2 Cor. 5: 10.   [2] 2 Cor. 13: 14.
[3] Matt. 6: vv. 9-13; Luke 11: vv. 2-4; *Book of Common Prayer.*

Priest

For thine is the kingdom, the power and the glory,[1] of the Father, and of the Son, and of the Holy Ghost; now, and for ever: world without end.

Peace unto all.

Deacon

Bow down your heads before the Lord.

Priest

O Master and Lord, the Father of mercies, and God of all comfort,[2] bless, hallow, guard, strengthen and stablish them that have bowed their heads unto thee. Turn them aside from every evil work:[3] to every good work unite them. And grant that they may partake without condemnation of these thy most pure and life-giving mysteries, for the remission of sins[4] and unto the communion of the Holy Ghost,[5]

Through the bountiful grace and love toward mankind of thine only-begotten Son, with whom thou art blessed together with thy most holy, good and life-giving Spirit; now, and for ever: world without end.

Choir

Amen

And unto thy spirit

To thee, O Lord

Amen

---

[1] Matt. 6: vv. 9–13; Luke 11: vv. 2–4; *Book of Common Prayer.*   [2] 2 Cor. 1: 3.   [3] 2 Tim. 4: 18.
[4] Matt. 26: 28.   [5] 2 Cor. 13: 14.

Give heed,[1] O Lord Jesus Christ, our God, from thy holy dwelling place,[2] and from the glorious throne of thy kingdom;[3] and come to sanctify us,[4] O thou that sittest on high with the Father and art here invisibly present with us. And vouchsafe by thy mighty hand[5] to impart unto us thy most pure body and precious blood; And through us unto all thy people.

The while the Priest is praying this prayer the Deacon standing before the Holy Doors shall gird his orarion about him crosswise. Then the Priest and the Deacon likewise in the place where he stands, bowing themselves shall repeat secretly, thrice,

O God, cleanse thou me a sinner, and be merciful to me.[6]

And when the Deacon seeth the Priest stretch forth his hands and touch the holy bread, to make the elevation, he shall say

Let us give heed.

And the Priest as he lifts up the holy bread shall say

The holy things[7] unto the holy.

Choir

One only is holy,[8] One only is the Lord,[9] Jesus Christ, to the glory of God the Father.[10] Amen

---

[1] Jer. 18: 19.   [2] 2 Chron. 30: 27; 1 Kings 8: 39.   [3] Song of the 3 Childr. v. 33.   [4] 1 Thess. 5: 23.
[5] Deut. 9: 26.   [6] Luke 18: 13.   [7] Ezek. 22: 26.   [8] Rev. 15: 4.   [9] Eph. 4: 5.   [10] Phil. 2: 11.

Then the Choir shall chant the anthem for the day [or of the Saint] the while the Deacon shall enter the sanctuary. And the Office continues as shewn for the Liturgy of S. John Chrysostom (pages 85-91).

When the Priest and the Deacon have partaken of the holy mysteries the Priest shall say silently

> We give thee thanks,[1] O Lord our God, for that thou hast suffered us to partake of thy holy, pure, immortal and heavenly mysteries unto the benefit, hallowing and healing of our souls and bodies. Do thou, O supreme Lord, grant that the communion of the body and blood of thy Christ be for us unto faith unashamed, unto love without dissimulation,[2] unto the increase of wisdom, unto the saving of soul and body, unto the driving out of every adversary, unto the fulfilling of thy commandments, and unto an acceptable defence at the dread judgment seat of thy Christ.[3]

And the rest as for the Liturgy of S. John Chrysostom (pages 92-8).

Then as the Reader reads Psalm 34 the Priest shall enter through the Holy Doors, and going to the offertory-table

Choir

---

[1] Rev. 11: 17.　　[2] Rom. 12: 9.　　[3] 2 Cor. 5: 10.

he shall say secretly this prayer the while the remainder of the holy things are being consumed

Accomplished and perfected in so far as lies in our power is all the mystery of thy dispensation, O Christ our God. For we have held in remembrance thy death; We have seen the figure of thy resurrection; We have been filled with thine immortal life. We have delighted in thine inexhaustible good pleasure, whereof be thou pleased to account us all worthy in the world to come, by the grace of thine eternal Father, and thy holy, good and life-giving Spirit; now, and for ever: world without end. Amen.

The while the Deacon going in by the north side shall consume the holy gifts with all reverence and care, the Priest shall come forth to distribute the anti-doron *to the people. When the Psalm is ended he shall say*

The blessing of the Lord be upon you, by his divine grace and loving-kindness, always, now, and for ever: world without end.

Glory be unto thee, O Christ our God and our hope,[1] glory be unto thee.

Choir

Amen

---

[1] 1 Tim. 1: 1.

Choir

Glory be unto the Father, and unto the Son, and unto the Holy Ghost; now, and for ever: world without end. Amen

Kyrie eleison [*thrice*]

Master, give the blessing

And a Dismissal is made

May Christ our true God [who is risen from the dead], by the prayers of his most holy Mother; by the power of the precious and life-giving cross; by the protection of the heavenly bodiless hosts; through the supplications of the glorious prophet and forerunner, John the Baptist; of the holy and all glorious apostles; of our sacred fathers among the Saints, the great hierarchs; of the holy, glorious and triumphant martyrs; of our sacred fathers whom God inspired; of the holy and righteous progenitors of God, Joachim and Anna; of our father among the saints, Basil the Great, archbishop of Caesarea in Cappadocia; of *N.* [*the saint to whom the church is dedicated*]; of *N.* to whose memory we dedicate this day; and of all the saints, have mercy upon us, and save our souls: For he is good and loving-kind.

Amen

The Priest now goeth into the sanctuary and saith the Prayers of Thanksgiving.[1] *After which he shall recite the Song of Simeon,*[2] *the* Trisagion, *and the rest, and the Lord's Prayer. And thereupon the Dismissal* troparion

Thy voice is gone out into all
   the earth,
O father among the saints,
Basil the Great, archbishop
of Caesarea in Cappadocia.
All peoples have received thy
   word,
wherewith thou didst teach
   fitly of God;
wherewith thou didst expound
the nature of all things;
and didst adorn the manners
   of men.

O holy father, royal priesthood,
pray to Christ our God
that our souls be saved.

   Glory be to the Father, and
to the Son, and to the Holy
Ghost;

And the kontakion

Rock-like foundation of the
   Church
hast thou shewn thyself,
dispensing unto all men
   dominion inviolate,
sealed by thy testimony,

Choir

---

[1] See page 211.   [2] *Nunc Dimittis*, Luke 2: vv. 29–32.

O Basil proven by heaven most holy.

Now, and for ever: world without end. Amen.

And the Hymn to the Mother of God
And the conclusion as on page 101

Choir

HERE ENDETH THE DIVINE LITURGY OF S. BASIL THE GREAT

THE
OFFICE
OF THE
DIVINE LITURGY
OF THE
PRESANCTIFIED GIFTS

During the Holy and Great Fast, when the Priest is to celebrate the Liturgy of the Presanctified, at the Office of Oblation (the Ordering) on the Sunday preceding he shall, after he hath cut the first altar-bread, and sacrificed and pierced it, as is appointed for the Liturgies of S. John Chrysostom and S. Basil the Great, cut other breads, saying over each of them these words following:

In remembrance: He was led: The Lamb of God: One of the soldiers:
[See pp. 23, 24]

Then he poureth the wine and water into the sacred chalice, pronouncing the customary words, and covereth them with the veil, and censeth them, repeating the Prayer of Oblation. Thereupon he beginneth the Divine Liturgy and celebrateth as is usual.

And when he is to sign the prosphora with the sign of the cross, at the invocation of the Holy Spirit, he saith **And make this bread:** *in the singular number, for Christ is one, and he doth not speak of* these breads, *in the plural number. And when he is to make the elevation he shall lift all the breads together, but break only the first bread that was offered and lay the portion in the holy chalice and pour in the warm water as is usual.*

Then taking the holy spoon in his right hand he dippeth it in the holy blood. With his left hand he taketh one of the breads and toucheth it with the holy spoon, which hath been wetted with the holy blood, making the sign of the cross over the cross that was cut earlier on the underside, and placeth it in the pyx. Then he doth the same with the other breads, and placeth them all in the pyx. Thereafter the Priest prayeth as is usual, and communicateth as is usual and performeth the Divine Liturgy according to the canon.

When the Priest is to celebrate the Liturgy of the Presanctified Gifts he entereth the sanctuary and vesteth himself, signing with the sign of the cross and kissing each vestment but saying nothing as he doth so, save **Let us pray unto the Lord** *over each of them.*

And the Deacon at a sign of blessing from the Priest goeth and taketh his stand at his appointed place, and exclaimeth **Master, give the blessing.** *And the Priest:* **Blessed is the kingdom of the Father, and of the Son, and of the Holy Ghost; now, and for ever: world without end.**

And straightway the Reader: **O come, let us worship** . . . *thrice. And there followeth the introductory Psalm. And in the mean while the Priest reciteth the Prayers of Light, that is, the Vesper Prayers, beginning with the fourth Prayer inasmuch as the first three are said after the litanies. And when the Psalm is done the Deacon beginneth the litany after the which there followeth Psalm 120:* **In my distress I cried unto the Lord** *and the other Psalms as appointed, with prostrations at the concluding* **Alleluia.**

Each of the antiphons is succeeded by the Short Litany offered by the Deacon with the concluding words pronounced by the Priest. At the opening of the Psalm the Priest shall go to the offertory-table. There he taketh the preconsecrated bread from the pyx and with all reverence placeth it on the holy paten, and poureth the wine and the water in the sacred chalice as is customary, saying naught. And taking the censer he censeth the asterisk *and the veils: and covereth the divine gifts, saying naught, not even the Prayer of Oblation but only* **By the prayers of our holy fathers, Lord Jesus Christ our God, have mercy upon us,** *for the Offering is already consecrated and complete.*

Following the reading from the Psalter, the chanting of **Lord, I cry unto thee:** *and the rest, Deacon and Priest make the Little Entrance without the* Book of the Gospels. *But when the Gospel is to be read, for the Feast-Day of a Saint or of the church, then the Entrance is made with the Holy Gospels.*

Deacon **Wisdom. Stand steadfast.**

And the Choir **O tender Light:**

Deacon **Let us give heed.**

Priest **Peace unto all.**

Deacon **Wisdom.**

And the Reader readeth the prokhimenon, *the Lesson from the* Book of Genesis, *and the second* prokhimenon.

And the Deacon   **Your bidding.**

And the Priest taking the censer and a lighted taper in his hands and standing before the altar and looking toward the east shall say as he maketh the sign of the cross   **Wisdom. Let us be upright.**

Likewise turning toward the west, toward the people   **The light of Christ lighteth every man.**

Reader   **The reading is from** *The Proverbs.*

Deacon   **Let us give heed.**

And the Reader readeth from the book of The Proverbs.

And the Priest after the reading   **Peace unto thee.**

Deacon   **Wisdom.**

And thereupon   **Let my prayer be set forth before thee as incense; and the lifting up of my hands as the evening sacrifice,** *the which the Choir repeateth.*

The Reader again   **Lord, I cry unto thee: make haste unto me; give ear unto my voice, when I cry unto thee.**

Choir   **Let my prayer:**

Reader   **Set a watch, O Lord, before my mouth; keep the door of my lips.**

Choir   **Let my prayer:**

Reader   **Incline not my heart to any evil thing, to practise wicked works with men that work iniquity.**

Choir   **Let my prayer:**

And again the Reader   **Let my prayer be set forth before thee as incense.**

And the Choir shall sing   **And the lifting up of my hands as the evening sacrifice.**

It is to be known that when the Reader singeth **Let my prayer be set forth before thee as incense** *all they that be present, in the church and in the sanctuary, shall kneel and pray. But when he beginneth* **And the lifting up of my hands:** *they shall rise. And the Priest standing in the sanctuary before the sacred altar shall take the censer with incense and cense. But when the Reader chanteth the final* **Let my prayer:** *then the Priest, handing the censer to the*

Deacon, shall bow his knee and pray. And at the end all present make three prostrations.

The Deacon now saith the Litany: And the rest.

At the Great Entrance **Now the heavenly powers:** *The prayer said in the other Liturgies during the singing of the* Cherubicon *is omitted. But the Priest as he censeth shall repeat Psalm 51. And after the divine mysteries have been brought forth to the chanting of* **Now the heavenly powers:** *three lowly reverences are to be made. The Priest now taketh the veils from the holy gifts and covereth them with the* aer. *And when the time is come to lift up the holy bread the holy gifts are not uncovered but with deep reverence and awe the Priest shall touch the divine bread beneath the veil that covereth them. The Deacon shall say* **Let us give heed.**

And the Priest in a loud voice:

The holy presanctified things unto the holy.

And the Divine Liturgy continueth according to the rubric, as shewn here in due time.

SOME FURTHER ANNOTATION
TO THE
CELEBRATION OF THE
LITURGY OF THE PRESANCTIFIED

The while the Choir singeth **Now the heavenly powers:** *Priest and Deacon go to the offertory-table, and taking up the* aer *the Priest placeth it on the Deacon's shoulder. But the sacred paten with the divine mysteries he lifteth with his right hand and placeth it on his own head; and taking the chalice with the wine in his left hand he holdeth it to his breast. And the Deacon, carrying only the censer, goeth before him, censing time and again. And during the Communion, after he hath proclaimed* **The holy presanctified things unto the holy** *the Priest layeth aside the* aer, *the Deacon entereth the sanctuary, and standing close to the Priest saith* **Break, O Master, the holy bread.** *And the Priest breaking it in four parts with all heedfulness shall say* **Broken and divided is the Lamb of God; Which being broken yet is not divided; Being ever eaten, never is consumed; But sanctifieth them that partake thereof.**

And he letteth fall the particle into the cup, saying naught; and the Deacon poureth the warm water into the cup, saying naught, and goeth to stand somewhat apart.

Now the Priest saith: **Deacon, draw near.**

And the Deacon shall approach and make a devout reverence, entreating forgiveness and saying:

Lo, I draw near unto our immortal King and God. *And:* **Impart unto me, O Master, the precious and holy body and blood of our Lord and God and Saviour Jesus Christ.**

And the Priest taking a single particle from the holy things giveth it to the Deacon saying:

Unto N., deacon in Holy Orders, is imparted the precious and holy and all pure body and blood of our Lord and God and Saviour Jesus Christ, for the remission of his sins and unto life everlasting.

And the Deacon having kissed the Priest's hand shall withdraw behind the sacred altar, and bowing his head he shall pray, as doth the Priest, saying **I believe, O Lord,** *and the rest.*

The Priest likewise taking a portion of the holy mysteries shall say **The precious and most holy body and blood of our Lord and God and Saviour Jesus Christ is imparted unto me, N., priest, for the remission of my sins and unto life everlasting.** *And bowing his head he shall pray saying* **I believe, O Lord, and confess:** *And* **Of thy mystical supper:** *And* **And let not this participation:** *to the end.*

And thus they partake of the holy mysteries in fear and with all precaution. Then the Priest shall take the spunge and spunge his hands, saying thrice **Glory be to thee, O God.**

And having kissed the spunge he shall return it to its place. Then he shall take the chalice with the veil in both hands and drink of it, saying nothing. And wiping his lips and the chalice with the veil in his hands he shall set it on the altar. And after he hath eaten his prosphoron *he shall perform the customary ablutions and thereafter still standing somewhat apart shall pray the Prayer of Thanksgiving:*

We give thee thanks, O God and Saviour of all men:

to the end. The Deacon shall not drink from the chalice at this time but after the prayer said by the Priest below the chancel steps, and after the remaining particles of the holy mysteries have been consumed. (But if the Priest celebrate alone, without a deacon, he likewise doth not drink from the chalice after his communion but after the Liturgy be finished, and after the holy mysteries have been consumed. For if the wine be sanctified by the placing in it of the particles, yet hath it not been transmade into the divine blood, seeing that the words of consecration are not recited over it in this service, as they are in the Liturgies of Basil the Great and John Chrysostom.) And the Deacon taking the sacred paten and approaching it to the sacred chalice putteth in the holy things, saying naught, and having made three reverences he openeth the Holy Doors.

THE
DIVINE OFFICE
OF THE
PRESANCTIFIED

The Deacon shall come out from the sanctuary to take his appointed place before the Holy Doors

And shall exclaim

Master, give the blessing.

The Priest, standing before the holy altar, shall say aloud

BLESSED is the kingdom of the Father, and of the Son, and of the Holy Ghost; now, and for ever: world without end.

Reader

Amen

O come, let us worship God our King. O come, let us worship and bow down[1] before Christ, our King and our God. O come, let us worship and bow down before the Very Christ, our King and our God.

Then shall follow the introductory Psalm [**Ps. 104**]

Bless the Lord, O my soul. O Lord my God, thou art very great; thou art clothed with honour and majesty.

---

[1] Ps. 95: 6.

Reader

Who coverest thyself with light as with a garment: who stretchest out the heavens like a curtain:

Who layeth the beams of his chambers in the waters: who maketh the clouds his chariot: who walketh upon the wings of the wind:

Who maketh his angels spirits; his ministers a flaming fire:

Who laid the foundations of the earth, that it should not be removed for ever.

Thou coveredst it with the deep as with a garment: the waters stood above the mountains.

At thy rebuke they fled; at the voice of thy thunder they hasted away.

They go up by the mountains; they go down by the valleys unto the place which thou hast founded for them.

Thou hast set a bound that they may not pass over; that they turn not again to cover the earth.

He sendeth the springs into the valleys, which run among the hills.

They give drink to every beast of the field: the wild asses quench their thirst.

By them shall the fowls of the heaven have their habitation, which sing among the branches.

He watereth the hills from his

Reader

chambers: the earth is satisfied with the fruit of thy works.

He causeth the grass to grow for the cattle, and herb for the service of man: that he may bring forth food out of the earth;

And wine that maketh glad the heart of man, and oil to make his face to shine, and bread which strengtheneth man's heart.

The trees of the Lord are full of sap; the cedars of Lebanon, which he hath planted;

Where the birds make their nests: as for the stork, the fir trees are her house.

The high hills are a refuge for the wild goats; and the rocks for the conies.

He appointed the moon for seasons: the sun knoweth his going down.

Thou makest darkness, and it is night: wherein all the beasts of the forest do creep forth.

The young lions roar after their prey, and seek their meat from God.

The sun ariseth, they gather themselves together, and lay them down in their dens.

Man goeth forth unto his work and to his labour until the evening.

O Lord, how manifold are thy works! in wisdom hast thou made

Reader

them all: the earth is full of thy riches.

So is this great and wide sea, wherein are things creeping innumerable, both small and great beasts.

There go the ships: there is that leviathan, whom thou hast made to play therein.

These wait all upon thee; that thou mayest give them their meat in due season.

That thou givest them they gather: thou openest thine hand, they are filled with good.

Thou hidest thy face, they are troubled: thou takest away their breath, they die, and return to their dust.

Thou sendest forth thy spirit, they are created: and thou renewest the face of the earth.

The glory of the Lord shall endure for ever: the Lord shall rejoice in his works.

He looketh on the earth, and it trembleth: he toucheth the hills, and they smoke.

I will sing unto the Lord as long as I live: I will sing praise to my God while I have my being.

My meditation of him shall be sweet: I will be glad in the Lord.

Let the sinners be consumed out of the earth, and let the wicked be no more. Bless thou the Lord, O my soul.

Reader

The sun knoweth his going down.[1]

Thou makest darkness, and it is night.[2]

O Lord, how manifold are thy works! in wisdom hast thou made them all.[3]

And then

Glory be to the Father, and to the Son, and to the Holy Ghost; now, and for ever: world without end. Amen.

Alleluia. Alleluia. Alleluia. Glory be to thee, O God. [*thrice*]

And in the mean while the Priest reciteth

The Vesper Prayers

O Thou unto whom the multitude of the heavenly host[4] doth sing eternal glory: Let our mouths be filled with thy praise[5] that we may magnify thy holy name. And grant unto us a portion and inheritance[6] with all them that fear thee in truth and keep thy commandments;[7] by the prayers of the holy Mother of God, and of all thy saints.

For unto thee belong all glory, honour and worship,

---

[1] Ps. 104: 19. [2] Ps. 104: 20. [3] Ps. 104: 24. [4] Luke 2: 13. [5] Ps. 71: 8.
[6] Ps. 16: 5. [7] Eccl. 12: 13.

unto the Father, and unto the Son, and unto the Holy Ghost; now, and for ever: world without end. Amen.

Lord, Lord, who upholdest all things in thy most pure hands; who art long-suffering unto us all and doth repent thee of our evils:[1] Remember thy tender mercies and thy loving-kindnesses.[2] Visit us with thy bounties and by thy grace keep us for the remainder of this day from the snares[3] of the devil, and preserve our lives from every wicked device;[4] by the grace of thy most holy Spirit.

Through the mercy and love toward mankind of thine only-begotten Son, with whom thou art blessed, together with thy most holy, good and life-giving Spirit; now, and for ever: world without end. Amen.

O great and wonderful God,[5] who of thine unsearchable goodness and rich providence dost order all things,[6] and hast bestowed on us the good of the land;[7] Who hast given us a pledge of the promised kingdom through the benefits already granted unto us, and to

Choir

---

[1] Joel 2: 13; Jonah 4: 2. [2] Ps. 25: 6. [3] Ps. 141: 9. [4] Ps. 140: 8.
[5] Daniel 9: 4 (*Septuagint*). [6] Wisdom 15: 1. [7] Isa. 1: 19.

Choir

this present hour hath caused evil to depart from us: Vouchsafe that we may complete the remainder of this day undefiled[1] before thy holy glory, and sing unto thee, Thou only who art good, our God which lovest mankind.

For thou art our God, and we ascribe glory to thee, to the Father, and to the Son, and to the Holy Ghost; now, and for ever: world without end. Amen.

O great and most high God, who only hath immortality, dwelling in light which no man can approach unto;[2] Who in wisdom didst make all thy works;[3] Who divided the light from the darkness;[4] Who made the sun to rule the day; Who made the moon and the stars to rule the night;[5] Who hast vouchsafed unto us sinners at this present hour to come before thy presence with thanksgiving,[6] and offer unto thee evening praise and glory: Do thou thyself of thy lovingkindness let our prayer be set before thee as incense,[7] and accept it for a sweetsmelling savour.[8] And grant that we may pass this eventide and the coming night in peace. Clothe

---

[1] Ps. 119: 1.   [2] 1 Tim. 6: 16.   [3] Ps. 104: 24.   [4] Gen. 1: 4.   [5] Gen. 1: 16;
Ps. 136: vv. 8–9.   [6] Ps. 95: 2.   [7] Ps. 141: 2.   [8] Eph. 5: 2.

us with the armour of light.[1]
Deliver us from the terror by
night,[2] from the pestilence
that walketh in darkness.[2]
Grant that the sleep which
thou hast appointed for the
repose of our weakness be
estranged[3] from all wicked
imaginations.[4] Yea, O Master,
Bestower of all blessings, may
we commune with our own
hearts upon our beds, and be
still[5] and call to remembrance
thy name in the night season:
That enlightened by meditation[6] of thy commandments[7]
we may rise up with joyful
soul[8] to glorify thy goodness,
with prayers and supplications
beseeching for thy mercy on
our own sins and for the sins of
all thy people, whom do thou
visit in clemency through
the intercessions of the holy
Mother of God.

For thou, O God, art good
and loving-kind; and we
ascribe glory to thee, to the
Father, and to the Son, and
to the Holy Ghost; now, and
for ever: world without end.
Amen.

Choir

---

[1] Rom. 13: 12.   [2] Ps. 91: vv. 5–6.   [3] Ps. 78: 30.   [4] Prov. 6: 18.   [5] Ps. 4: 4.
[6] Ps. 49: 3.   [7] Ps. 119: vv. 97–8.   [8] Ps. 35: 9.

And when the Psalm is finished the Deacon saith

The Great Litany

In peace let us pray unto the Lord,

For the peace from on high, and for the salvation of our souls, let us pray unto the Lord,

For the peace and union of the whole world, and for the good estate of the holy churches of God, let us pray unto the Lord,

For this holy temple and for them that enter therein with faith, reverence and fear of God, let us pray unto the Lord,

For our Patriarch N.; for the honourable order of priesthood; and for the diaconate which is in Christ; For all the clergy and the people, let us pray unto the Lord,

For our Sovereign Lady, Queen Elizabeth [*or the Civil Authority*]; For this country, and for those in authority over us, let us pray unto the Lord,

For this city [*or* monastery]; For every city and land, and for them that dwell therein with faith, let us pray unto the Lord,

For fair seasons and for an abundance of the fruits of the earth, let us pray unto the Lord,

For them that travel by land, by water, by air; For the sick and the suffering; For those in cap-

Choir

Kyrie eleison

tivity, And for their salvation, let us pray unto the Lord,

That we may be delivered from all tribulation, wrath, danger and necessity, let us pray unto the Lord,

Succour, save, comfort and preserve us, O God, by thy grace,

Mindful of our most holy and undefiled, most blessed and glorious Lady, Mother of God and ever-Virgin Mary; and of all the saints; Let us commend ourselves, and one another, and our whole life to Christ our God,

Priest

For unto thee belong all glory, honour and worship, unto the Father, and unto the Son, and unto the Holy Ghost; now, and for ever: world without end.

Choir

To thee, O Lord

Amen

And the Reader shall read

Psalm 120

In my distress I cried unto the Lord, and he heard me.

Deliver my soul, O Lord, from lying lips, and from a deceitful tongue.

What shall be given unto thee? or what shall be done unto thee, thou false tongue?

Sharp arrows of the mighty, with coals of juniper.

Woe is me, that I sojourn in Mesech, that I dwell in the tents of Kedar!

Reader

My soul hath long dwelt with him that hateth peace.

I am for peace: but when I speak, they are for war.

And *Psalm 121*

I will lift up mine eyes unto the hills, from whence cometh my help.

My help cometh from the Lord, which made heaven and earth.

He will not suffer thy foot to be moved: he that keepeth thee will not slumber.

Behold, he that keepeth Israel shall neither slumber nor sleep.

The Lord is thy keeper: the Lord is thy shade upon thy right hand.

The sun shall not smite thee by day, nor the moon by night.

The Lord shall preserve thee from all evil: he shall preserve thy soul.

The Lord shall preserve thy going out and thy coming in from this time forth, and even for evermore.

And *Psalm 122*

I was glad when they said unto me, Let us go into the house of the Lord.

Our feet shall stand within thy gates, O Jerusalem.

Jerusalem is builded as a city that is compact together:

Reader

Whither the tribes go up, the tribes of the Lord, unto the testimony of Israel, to give thanks unto the name of the Lord.

For there are set thrones of judgment, the thrones of the House of David.

Pray for the peace of Jerusalem: they shall prosper that love thee.

Peace be within thy walls, and prosperity within thy palaces.

For my brethren and companions' sakes, I will now say, Peace be within thee.

Because of the house of the Lord our God I will seek thy good.

And **Psalm *123***

Unto thee lift I up mine eyes, O thou that dwellest in the heavens.

Behold, as the eyes of servants look unto the hand of their masters, and as the eyes of a maiden unto the hand of her mistress; so our eyes wait upon the Lord our God, until that he have mercy upon us.

Have mercy upon us, O Lord, have mercy upon us: for we are exceedingly filled with contempt.

Our soul is exceedingly filled with the scorning of those that are at ease, and with the contempt of the proud.

Reader

And **Psalm 124**

If it had not been the Lord who was on our side, now may Israel say;

If it had not been the Lord who was on our side, when men rose up against us:

Then they had swallowed us up quick, when their wrath was kindled against us:

Then the waters had over-whelmed us, the stream had gone over our soul:

Then the proud waters had gone over our soul.

Blessed be the Lord, who hath not given us as a prey to their teeth.

Our soul is escaped as a bird out of the snare of the fowlers: the snare is broken, and we are escaped.

Our help is in the name of the Lord, who made heaven and earth.

And then

Glory be to the Father, and to the Son, and to the Holy Ghost; now, and for ever: world without end. Amen.

Alleluia. Alleluia. Alleluia. Glory be to thee, O God. [*thrice*]

And in the mean while the Priest prayeth

The Prayer of the First Antiphon

O Lord who art gracious and full of compassion;[1] long-suffering and plenteous in mercy:[2] Give ear to our prayer,[3] and attend to the voice of our supplications.[4] Shew us a token for good.[5] Teach us thy way, that we may walk in thy truth.[6] Rejoice our hearts to fear thy holy name. For thou art great, and doest wondrous things. Thou art God alone,[7] and there is none like unto thee,[8] O Lord, among the gods, mighty in mercy, gracious[9] in strength to succour, comfort and save all who put their trust in thy holy name.

Deacon

Again and again in peace let us pray unto the Lord,

Succour, save, comfort and preserve us, O God, by thy grace,

Mindful of our most holy and undefiled, most blessed and glorious Lady, Mother of God and ever-Virgin Mary; and of all the saints; Let us commend ourselves, and one another, and our whole life to Christ our God,

Choir

Kyrie eleison

To thee, O Lord

---

[1] Ps. 111: 4. [2] Ps. 86: 15. [3] Ps. 55: 1. [4] Ps. 86: 6. [5] Ps. 86: 17. [6] Ps. 86: 11.
[7] Ps. 86: 10. [8] Ps. 86: 8. [9] 1 Pet. 2: 3.

Priest

For thine is the might, thine the kingdom, the power and the glory, of the Father, and of the Son, and of the Holy Ghost; now, and for ever: world without end.

Choir

Amen

And the Reader shall read

Psalm 125

They that trust in the Lord shall be as mount Zion, which cannot be removed, but abideth for ever.

As the mountains are round about Jerusalem, so the Lord is round about his people from henceforth even for ever.

For the rod of the wicked shall not rest upon the lot of the righteous; lest the righteous put forth their hands unto iniquity.

Do good, O Lord, unto those that be good, and to them that are upright in their hearts.

And as for such as turn aside unto their crooked ways, the Lord shall lead them forth with the workers of iniquity: but peace shall be upon Israel.

And Psalm 126

When the Lord turned again the captivity of Zion, we were like them that dream.

Then was our mouth filled with laughter, and our tongue with singing: then said they among the heathen, The Lord hath done great things for them.

Reader

The Lord hath done great things for us; whereof we are glad.

Turn again our captivity, O Lord, as the streams in the south.

They that sow in tears shall reap in joy.

He that goeth forth and weepeth, bearing precious seed, shall doubtless come again with rejoicing, bringing his sheaves with him.

And **Psalm 127**

Except the Lord build the house, they labour in vain that build it: except the Lord keep the city, the watchman waketh but in vain.

It is vain for you to rise up early, to sit up late, to eat the bread of sorrows: for so he giveth his beloved sleep.

Lo, children are an heritage of the Lord: and the fruit of the womb is his reward.

As arrows are in the hand of a mighty man; so are children of the youth.

Happy is the man that hath his quiver full of them: they shall not be ashamed, but they shall speak with the enemies in the gate.

And **Psalm 128**

Blessed is every one that feareth the Lord; that walketh in his ways.

Reader

For thou shalt eat the labour of thine hands: happy shalt thou be, and it shall be well with thee.

Thy wife shall be as a fruitful vine by the sides of thine house: thy children like olive plants round about thy table.

Behold, that thus shall the man be blessed that feareth the Lord.

The Lord shall bless thee out of Zion: and thou shalt see the good of Jerusalem all the days of thy life.

Yea, thou shalt see thy children's children, and peace upon Israel.

And **Psalm 129**

Many a time have they afflicted me from my youth, may Israel now say:

Many a time have they afflicted me from my youth: yet they have not prevailed against me.

The plowers plowed upon my back: they made long their furrows.

The Lord is righteous: he hath cut asunder the cords of the wicked.

Let them all be confounded and turned back that hate Zion.

Let them be as the grass upon the housetops, which withereth afore it groweth up:

Wherewith the mower filleth

not his hand; nor he that bindeth sheaves his bosom.

Neither do they which go by say, The blessing of the Lord be upon you: we bless you in the name of the Lord.

And then

Glory be to the Father, and to the Son, and to the Holy Ghost; now, and for ever: world without end. Amen.

Alleluia. Alleluia. Alleluia. Glory be to thee, O God. [*thrice*]

And in the mean while the Priest prayeth

The Prayer of the Second Antiphon

O Lord, rebuke us not in thy wrath; neither chasten us in thy hot displeasure:[1] But deal with us according unto thy mercy,[2] O Physician and Healer of our souls, who dost lead us into the haven[3] of thy will. Enlighten the eyes of our understanding[4] to the knowledge of thy truth; and grant that the remainder of this day, and our whole life, may be peaceful and without sin, by the prayers of the holy Mother of God, and of all thy saints.

---

[1] Ps. 38: 1.   [2] Ps. 119: 124.   [3] Ps. 107: 30.   [4] Eph. 1: 18.

Deacon

Again and again in peace let us pray unto the Lord,

Succour, save, comfort and preserve us, O God, by thy grace,

Mindful of our most holy and undefiled, most blessed and glorious Lady, Mother of God and ever-Virgin Mary; and of all the saints; Let us commend ourselves, and one another, and our whole life to Christ our God,

Priest

For thou, O God, art good and loving-kind, and we ascribe glory to thee, to the Father, and to the Son, and to the Holy Ghost; now, and for ever: world without end.

Choir

Kyrie eleison

To thee, O Lord

Amen

And the Reader shall continue

Psalm 130

Out of the depths have I cried unto thee, O Lord.

Lord, hear my voice: let thine ears be attentive to the voice of my supplications.

If thou, Lord, shouldest mark iniquities, O Lord, who shall stand?

But there is forgiveness with thee, that thou mayest be feared.

I wait for the Lord, my soul doth wait, and in his word do I hope.

My soul waiteth for the Lord more than they that watch for

Reader

the morning: I say, more than they that watch for the morning.

Let Israel hope in the Lord: for with the Lord there is mercy, and with him is plenteous redemption.

And he shall redeem Israel from all his iniquities.

And **Psalm** *131*

Lord, my heart is not haughty, nor mine eyes lofty: neither do I exercise myself in great matters, or in things too high for me.

Surely I have behaved and quieted myself, as a child that is weaned of his mother: my soul is even as a weaned child.

Let Israel hope in the Lord from henceforth and for ever.

And **Psalm** *132*

Lord, remember David, and all his afflictions:

How he sware unto the Lord, and vowed unto the mighty God of Jacob;

Surely I will not come into the tabernacle of my house, nor go up into my bed;

I will not give sleep to mine eyes, or slumber to mine eyelids,

Until I find out a place for the Lord, an habitation for the mighty God of Jacob.

Reader

Lo, we heard of it at Ephratah: we found it in the fields of the wood.

We will go into his tabernacles: we will worship at his footstool.

Arise, O Lord, into thy rest; thou, and the ark of thy strength.

Let thy priests be clothed with righteousness; and let thy saints shout for joy.

For thy servant David's sake turn not away the face of thine anointed.

The Lord hath sworn in truth unto David; he will not turn from it; Of the fruit of thy body will I set upon thy throne.

If thy children will keep my covenant and my testimony that I shall teach them, their children shall also sit upon thy throne for evermore.

For the Lord hath chosen Zion; he hath desired it for his habitation.

This is my rest for ever: here will I dwell; for I have desired it.

I will abundantly bless her provision: I will satisfy her poor with bread.

I will also clothe her priests with salvation: and her saints shall shout aloud for joy.

There will I make the horn of David to bud: I have ordained a lamp for mine anointed.

Reader

His enemies will I clothe with shame: but upon himself shall his crown flourish.

And **Psalm 133**

Behold, how good and how pleasant it is for brethren to dwell together in unity!

It is like the precious ointment upon the head, that ran down upon the beard, even Aaron's beard: that went down to the skirts of his garments;

As the dew of Hermon, and as the dew that descended upon the mountains of Zion: for there the Lord commanded the blessing, even life for evermore.

And **Psalm 134**

Behold, bless ye the Lord, all ye servants of the Lord, which by night stand in the house of the Lord.

Lift up your hands in the sanctuary, and bless the Lord.

The Lord that made heaven and earth bless thee out of Zion.

And then

Glory be to the Father, and to the Son, and to the Holy Ghost; now, and for ever: world without end. Amen.

Alleluia. Alleluia. Alleluia. Glory be to thee, O God. [*thrice*]

And in the mean while the Priest prayeth

The Prayer of the Third Antiphon

O Lord our God, remember us sinners and thine unprofitable servants,[1] when we call upon thy holy and honoured name, and confound not our expectation[2] of thy mercy; But fulfil, O Lord, all our petitions which are unto salvation, and vouchsafe that we may love and fear thee with our whole heart, and do thy will in all things.

Deacon

Again and again in peace let us pray unto the Lord,

    Succour, save, comfort and preserve us, O God, by thy grace,

    Mindful of our most holy and undefiled, most blessed and glorious Lady, Mother of God and ever-Virgin Mary; and of all the saints; Let us commend ourselves and one another, and our whole life to Christ our God,

Priest

For thou art our God, the God of mercy and salvation, and unto thee do we ascribe glory, unto the Father, and unto the Son, and unto the Holy Ghost; now, and for ever: world without end.

Choir

Kyrie eleison

To thee, O Lord

Amen

---

[1] Matt. 25: 30.   [2] Ps. 62: 5.

And the Choir shall sing

Psalm 141

Lord, I cry unto thee: make haste unto me.

Make haste unto me, O Lord.

Lord, I cry unto thee: make haste unto me; give ear unto my voice, when I cry unto thee.

Make haste unto me, O Lord.

Let my prayer be set forth before thee as incense; and the lifting up of my hands as the evening sacrifice.

Make haste unto me, O Lord.

Set a watch, O Lord, before my mouth; keep the door of my lips.

Incline not my heart to any evil thing, to practise wicked works with men that work iniquity: and let me not eat of their dainties.

Let the righteous smite me; it shall be a kindness; and let him reprove me; it shall be an excellent oil, which shall not break my head: for yet my prayer also shall be in their calamities.

When their judges are overthrown in stony places, they shall hear my words; for they are sweet.

Our bones are scattered at the grave's mouth, as when one cutteth and cleaveth wood upon the earth.

But mine eyes are unto thee, O God the Lord: in thee is my trust; leave not my soul destitute.

Keep me from the snares which

Choir

they have laid for me, and the gins of the workers of iniquity.

Let the wicked fall into their own nets, whilst that I withal escape.

And **Psalm 142**

I cried unto the Lord with my voice; with my voice unto the Lord did I make my supplication.

I poured out my complaint before him; I shewed before him my trouble.

When my spirit was overwhelmed within me, then thou knewest my path. In the way wherein I walked have they privily laid a snare for me.

I looked on my right hand, and beheld, but there was no man that would know me: refuge failed me; no man cared for my soul.

I cried unto thee, O Lord: I said, Thou art my refuge and my portion in the land of the living.

Attend unto my cry; for I am brought very low: deliver me from my persecutors; for they are stronger than I.

*   *   *   *

Bring my soul out of prison, that I may praise thy name:
The righteous shall compass

Choir

me about; for thou shalt deal bountifully with me.

* * * *

Psalm 130

Out of the depths have I cried unto thee, O Lord. Lord, hear my voice:

Let thine ears be attentive to the voice of my supplications.

* * * *

If thou, Lord, shouldest mark iniquities, O Lord, who shall stand? But there is forgiveness with thee, that thou mayest be feared.

I wait for the Lord, my soul doth wait, and in his word do I hope. My soul waiteth for the Lord.

* * * *

More than they that watch for the morning: I say, more than they that watch for the morning. Let Israel hope in the Lord:

For with the Lord there is mercy, and with him is plenteous redemption. And he shall redeem Israel from all his iniquities.

Psalm 117

O praise the Lord, all ye nations: praise him, all ye people.

For his merciful kindness is

Choir

great toward us: and the truth of the Lord endureth for ever.

And then

Glory be to the Father, and to the Son, and to the Holy Ghost; now, and for ever: world without end. Amen.

And the Deacon censeth the sanctuary and the ikonostasis and the congregation present.

Then the Priest and the Deacon with the censer make the Little Entrance. But when the Gospel is to be read (for the Feast-Day of a Saint or of the church) then the Entrance is made with the Holy Gospels.

Priest

Prayer of the Entrance

Evening, and morning, and at noon[1] we praise thee, we bless thee, we give thanks unto thee, and we pray unto thee, O Master of all: Let our prayer be set forth before thee as incense;[2] and incline not our hearts to any evil thing.[3] But keep us from all who would lay a snare[4] for our souls; For our eyes wait upon thee, O Lord.[5] In thee, O Lord, is our trust.[6] Confound us not, O God.

---

[1] Ps. 55: 17. [2] Ps. 141: 2. [3] Ps. 141: 4. [4] Ps. 141: 9. [5] Ps. 123: 2. [6] Ps. 141: 8.

Choir

For unto thee belong all glory, honour and worship, unto the Father, and unto the Son, and unto the Holy Ghost; now, and for ever: world without end. Amen.

After the canticles the Deacon or the Priest shall proclaim

Wisdom. Stand steadfast.

And the Choir shall sing

O tender Light of the glory of the
    Father immortal,
Heavenly, holy and blessed, O
    Jesus Christ.
Come now at the setting of the
    sun,
We see the lights of eventide
    around us shine,
And hymn the Father, Son and
    Holy Spirit: God.
Meet it is that at all times thou
    shouldest be praised
By voices pure and undefiled,
    O Son of God, Giver of life.
Wherefore all the world doth
    glorify thee.

Deacon

Let us give heed.

Priest

Peace unto all.

Deacon

Wisdom.

And the Reader readeth the pro-khimenon for the day; the Lesson from the Book of Genesis; and the second prokhimenon.

Deacon

Your bidding.

And thereupon the Priest, holding a lighted taper and the censer in his hands, exclaimeth aloud, looking toward the east

Wisdom. Let us be upright.

Likewise, turned toward the west, to the congregation, he saith

The light of Christ lighteth every man.[1]

And the Reader readeth from the Old Testament.

[If the morrow be a Feast-Day the reading from the Old Testament is now followed by the readings appointed for the Feast.]

After the which

Let my prayer be set forth before thee as incense; and the lifting up of my hands as the evening sacrifice.[2]

Choir

Let my prayer be set forth before thee as incense; and the lifting up of my hands as the evening sacrifice

---

[1] John 1: 9.   [2] Ps. 141: 2.

Reader	*Choir*
Lord, I cry unto thee: make haste unto me; give ear unto my voice, when I cry unto thee.[1]	
	Let my prayer be set forth before thee as incense; and the lifting up of my hands as the evening sacrifice
Set a watch, O Lord, before my mouth; keep the door of my lips.	
	Let my prayer be set forth before thee as incense; and the lifting up of my hands as the evening sacrifice
Incline not my heart to any evil thing, to practise wicked works with men that work iniquity.	
	Let my prayer be set forth before thee as incense; and the lifting up of my hands as the evening sacrifice
Let my prayer be set forth before thee as incense.	
	And the lifting up of my hands as the evening sacrifice
Priest	
The Prayer of S. Ephraim the Syrian	
O Lord and Master of my life, Take from me the spirit of sloth, Of despondency, of lust for power, Of vain speaking.	

---

[1] Ps. 141: vv. 1-4.

But the spirit of integrity,
Of humility, of patience and love
Grant thou unto me, thy servant.

Yea, Lord and King,
Give me awareness of my own
sins,
And let me not judge my brother,
For blessed art thou for ever and
ever. Amen.

[If it be the Feast-Day of a Saint, or of
the church, then the Deacon or the
Priest shall say

Let us give heed.

And the Reader shall read the prokhimenon *of the Epistle.*

The Epistle is read, the Alleluia is
chanted, and the Gospel is read.]

The Deacon beginneth the Litany

Let us all say with our whole soul,
and with our whole mind, let
us say,
   O Almighty Lord, God of our
fathers, we pray thee, hear and
have mercy,
   Have mercy upon us, O God,
after thy great goodness. We pray
thee, hear and have mercy,
   We beseech thee also for our
Patriarch N.; for all priests and
religious; and for all our brethren
in Christ,
   We beseech thee also for our
Sovereign Lady, Queen Elizabeth
[*or the Civil Authority*], and for all
that are in authority; That we

Choir

Kyrie eleison

Kyrie eleison   [*thrice*]

may lead a quiet and peaceable life in all godliness and honesty,[1]

We beseech thee also for blessed and ever-memorable holy Orthodox patriarchs; for pious kings and devout queens; for the founders of this holy church [*or* monastery]; And for all thy servants who have departed this life in faith and are now at rest,

We beseech thee also for grace, life, peace, health and salvation for the servants of God *** *** ***,

We beseech thee also for them that strive[2] and bring forth the fruit of good works in this holy and venerable temple; for them that serve and them that sing; And for all the people here present who await thy great and bountiful mercy,

During the Litany the Priest shall say

The Prayer of Fervent Supplication

O Lord our God, accept this fervent supplication from thy servants, and have mercy upon us according unto the multitude[3] of thy mercies; And send down thy bounties upon us and upon all thy people which look unto thee for plenteous mercy.[4]

Choir

---

[1] 1 Tim. 2: 2. [2] Phil. 1: 27. [3] Ps. 51: 1. [4] Ps. 86: 5; 103: 8.

For thou, O God, art gracious[1] and full of compassion, and unto thee we ascribe glory, unto the Father, and unto the Son, and unto the Holy Spirit; now, and for ever: world without end.

Choir

Amen

Deacon

Catechumens, pray ye unto the Lord,

Let us, the faithful, pray for the catechumens, that the Lord may have mercy upon them,

That he may instruct them in the word of truth,

That he may reveal unto them the gospel of righteousness,

That he may unite them to his Holy, Catholick and Apostolick Church,

Save them. Have mercy upon them. Protect and preserve them, O God, by thy grace,

Ye catechumens, bow your heads unto the Lord,

Kyrie eleison

To thee, O Lord

Priest

The Prayer for the Catechumens

O God, our God, Creator and Author of all things; Who willest that all should be saved, and come unto the knowledge of the truth:[2] Cast thine eyes upon thy servants

---

[1] 1 Pet. 2: 3.   [2] 1 Tim. 2: 4.

the catechumens, and deliver them from their ancient errors and from the wiles of the adversary: And call them unto life eternal, enlightning their souls and bodies, and numbering them among thy reasonable flock on which is named thy holy name,[1]

That they also with us may glorify thy sublime and wondrous name, of the Father, and of the Son, and of the Holy Ghost; now, and for ever: world without end.

Choir

Amen

And the Deacon shall say

All ye that are catechumens, depart. Catechumens, depart. All ye catechumens, depart. Let not any of the catechumens remain. All we the faithful, again and again in peace let us pray unto the Lord,

Kyrie eleison

From the Wednesday after the third Sunday in Lent in the place of the above exhortation to the catechumens to depart the Deacon shall exhort and pray thus for them that are to be baptized at the forthcoming Easter

Catechumens, depart. Catechumens, depart. All ye that are to be illuminated,[2] draw near. Pray, all ye that are to be illuminated.

Kyrie eleison

---

[1] Gen. 48: 16.   [2] Heb. 10: 32.

Ye faithful, for these brethren that are preparing for holy illumination, and for their salvation, let us pray unto the Lord,

That the Lord our God may stablish them and strengthen them,

That he will enlighten them with the illumination of knowledge and godliness,

That he will vouchsafe unto them in his own good time the washing of regeneration,[1] the remission of sins,[2] and the garment of incorruption,

That they may be born again of water and the Spirit,

That he will grant unto them the perfection of faith,

That he will number them with his holy and chosen flock,

Save them. Have mercy upon them. Protect and preserve them, O God, by thy grace,

Ye that do prepare for illumination, bow your heads unto the Lord,

Choir

To thee, O Lord

The Priest here saith silently

The Prayer for them that are preparing for Holy Illumination

Reveal thy countenance, O Lord, unto them that are preparing for holy illumination, and who desire to cast off the

---

[1] Titus 3: 5.   [2] Matt. 26: 28.

filthiness of sin. Illumine their understanding. Stablish them in faith. Confirm them in hope. Perfect them in charity. Make them honourable members[1] of thy Christ, who gave himself a ransom for our souls.[2]

For thou art our illumination, and unto thee we ascribe glory, unto the Father, and unto the Son, and unto the Holy Spirit; now, and for ever: world without end.

Choir

Amen

Deacon

As many as are to be illuminated, depart. Depart, ye that are preparing for illumination. Catechumens, depart. Let not any of the catechumens remain. All we the faithful, again and again in peace let us pray unto the Lord,

Kyrie eleison

Here endeth the exhortation to them that are preparing for baptism that is added to the Liturgy from the Wednesday after the third Sunday in Lent.

The Priest saith silently

The First Prayer of the Faithful

O God, great and greatly to be praised,[3] who through the life-giving death of thy Christ hast

---

[1] 1 Cor. 12: 23.   [2] Exod. 30: 12; 1 Tim. 2: 6.   [3] Ps. 48: 1.

translated us[1] from corruption to incorruption: Deliver all our senses from their vile affections[2] that bring forth fruit unto death,[3] making the inner man[4] to have dominion over them: And let our eye be blind to every evil sight. Let our ear be deaf to all idle words, our tongue be purged from unseemly speech. Purify our lips that praise thee, O Lord. Cause our hands to abstain from sinful deeds and to do only those things that are pleasing in thy sight,[5] stablishing all our members and our minds by thy grace.

Choir

Deacon

Succour, save, comfort and preserve us, O God, by thy grace, Wisdom.

Kyrie eleison

Priest

For unto thee belong all glory, honour and worship, unto the Father, and unto the Son, and unto the Holy Ghost; now, and for ever: world without end.

Amen

Deacon

Again and again in peace let us pray unto the Lord,

Kyrie eleison

---

[1] Col. 1: 13.   [2] Rom. 1: 26.   [3] Rom. 7: 5.   [4] Eph. 3: 16.   [5] 1 John 3: 22.

For the peace from on high, and for the salvation of our souls, let us pray unto the Lord,

For the peace and union of the whole world, and for the good estate of the holy churches of God, let us pray unto the Lord,

For this holy temple and for them that enter therein with faith, reverence and fear of God, let us pray unto the Lord,

That we may be delivered from all tribulation, wrath, danger and necessity, let us pray unto the Lord,

The Priest meanwhile shall say

The Second Prayer of the Faithful

O Master, holy and exceeding good, we pray thee who art rich in mercy,[1] be merciful unto us sinners, and make us worthy to receive thine only-begotten Son and our God, the King of glory.[2] For behold, his most pure body and life-giving blood, entering at this present hour, are about to be laid upon this mystical altar, invisibly attended by the multitude of the heavenly host.[3] Grant that we may partake of them without condemnation; that the eyes of our understanding

Choir

---

[1] Eph. 2: 4. [2] Ps. 24: vv. 7-10. [3] Luke 2: 13.

being enlightened[1] thereby we may become children of light and of the day.[2]

Deacon

Succour, save, comfort and preserve us, O God, by thy grace, Wisdom.

Priest

According to the gift[3] of thy Christ, with whom thou art blessed together with thy most holy, good and life-giving Spirit; now, and for ever: world without end.

And the while the anthem is being sung the Deacon entereth the sanctuary through the north door to cense the sacred altar and the offertory-table and the Priest.

Choir

Kyrie eleison

Amen

In the place of the Cherubicon *the Choir shall sing*

Now the heavenly powers invisibly do minister with us: For lo, the King of glory[4] entereth. Behold, the mystical sacrifice all accomplished is borne on high. In faith and love let us draw near that we may become partakers of eternal life.

Alleluia. Alleluia. Alleluia.

---

[1] Eph. 1: 18.   [2] 1 Thess. 5: 5.   [3] Eph. 3: 7.   [4] Ps. 24: vv. 7–10.

And together they stand and repeat three times **Now the heavenly powers,** *and the rest.*

And having made three lowly reverences they go in silence to bring forth the holy gifts as prescribed. And the Priest in the usual manner shall lay the divine mysteries on the altar and, still silent, shall cover them with the aer *and cense them only.*

*

The Deacon likewise at a sign of blessing from the Priest proceedeth to his accustomed place and saith

Let us complete our evening supplication unto the Lord,

For the precious and presanctified gifts here set forth, let us pray unto the Lord,

That our God which loveth mankind; Who hath received them unto his holy and heavenly altar for a sweetsmelling savour[1] of spiritual fragrance may send down upon us divine grace and the gift of the Holy Spirit, let us pray unto the Lord,

That we may be delivered from all tribulation, wrath, danger and necessity, let us pray unto the Lord,

The Priest prayeth

O God of ineffable mysteries in whom are hid the treasures

Choir

Kyrie eleison

---

* *Here shall follow the Ordering of Deacons.*   [1] Eph. 5: 2.

of wisdom and knowledge;[1] Who hast revealed unto us the service of this ministry, and of thy great love toward mankind hast appointed us sinners to offer unto thee gifts and sacrifices for our sins and for the errors of the people:[2] Do thou, O invisible King, that performest things[3] great and searchless, glorious and excellent: they are more than can be numbered:[4] look down upon us, thine unworthy servants who stand before this sacred altar, as before thy mercy seat between the cherubims,[5] where lieth thine only-begotten Son and our God in the dread mysteries that rest thereon; and having saved us and thy faithful people from all our uncleannesses,[6] hallow our souls and bodies with the sanctification which cannot be taken away. That partaking with a pure conscience, with face not ashamed,[7] with an enlightened heart of these divine gifts, and being quickened by them, we may be united unto thy Christ himself, our true God, who hath said: He that eateth my flesh, and drinketh my blood, dwelleth in me, and

Choir

---

[1] Col. 2: 3.   [2] Heb. 9: 7, 9.   [3] Ps. 57: 2.   [4] Ps. 40: 5.   [5] Exod. 25: 22.   [6] Ezek. 36: 29.
[7] Ps. 34: 5.

I in him;[1] That with thy word, O Lord, dwelling in us, and walking in us[2] we may become the temple of thy holy and ever venerated Spirit, redeemed from every snare of the devil,[3] manifest in deed or word or thought; and may obtain the good things promised unto us, with all thy saints who since the world began have been pleasing in thy sight.[4]

Choir

Deacon

Succour, save, comfort and preserve us, O God, by thy grace,

That this whole eventide may be perfect, holy, peaceful and without sin, let us entreat the Lord,

For an angel of peace, faithful guide and guardian of our souls and bodies, let us entreat the Lord,

For pardon and remission of our sins and transgressions, let us entreat the Lord,

For things good and profitable to our souls, and peace for the world, let us entreat the Lord,

That we may pass the remainder of our lives in peace and repentance, let us entreat the Lord,

For a Christian ending to our life, painless, without shame and

Kyrie eleison

Grant us, O Lord

---

[1] John 6: 56.   [2] 2 Cor. 6: 16.   [3] 1 Tim. 3: 7.   [4] 1 John 3: 22.

peaceful, and a good defence before the dread judgment seat of Christ,[1] let us entreat the Lord,

Having besought the unity of the faith and the communion of the Holy Ghost,[2] let us commend ourselves, and one another, and our whole life to Christ our God,

Priest

And vouchsafe, O Lord, that boldly and without condemnation we may dare to lift our voices unto thee, O heavenly God and Father, and say

For thine is the kingdom, the power and the glory,[3] of the Father, and of the Son, and of the Holy Ghost; now, and for ever: world without end.

    Peace unto all.

Choir

To thee, O Lord

Our Father which art in heaven,
Hallowed be thy Name,
Thy kingdom come,
Thy will be done, in earth
as it is in heaven.
Give us this day our daily bread;
And forgive us our trespasses,
As we forgive them that trespass against us;
And lead us not into temptation,
But deliver us from evil.[3]

Amen

And unto thy spirit

---

[1] 2 Cor. 5: 10.   [2] 2 Cor. 13: 14.   [3] Matt. 6: vv. 9–13; Luke 11: vv. 2–4; *Book of Common Prayer*.

Deacon	*Choir*
Let us bow down our heads before the Lord.	To thee, O Lord

The Priest bowing his head prayeth in a low voice

> O God who alone art good and full of compassion; Who dwellest in the heights and dost look down in mercy on the humble of heart: Turn the eye of thy loving-kindness upon all thy people, and preserve them;[1] And grant that all we may partake without condemnation of these thy life-giving mysteries: For unto thee have we bowed our heads, in the earnest expectation[2] of thy bountiful mercy,

Through the bountiful grace and love toward mankind of thine only-begotten Son, with whom thou art blessed together with thy most holy, good and life-giving Spirit; now, and for ever: world without end.

Amen

The Priest prayeth secretly

> Give heed,[3] O Lord Jesus Christ, our God, from thy holy dwelling place,[4] and from the glorious throne of thy kingdom;[5] and come to sanctify us,[6] O thou that sittest on high

---

[1] Ps. 40: 11.   [2] Phil. 1: 20; Rom. 8: 19.   [3] Jer. 18: 19.   [4] 2 Chron. 30: 27; 1 Kings 8: 39.
[5] Song of the 3 Childr. v. 33.   [6] 1 Thess. 5: 23.

with the Father and art here invisibly present with us. And vouchsafe by thy mighty hand[1] to impart unto us of thy most pure body and precious blood; And through us unto all thy people.

And after the Prayer the Priest and the Deacon bow themselves thrice saying

O God, cleanse thou me, a sinner.

Then the Priest with deep reverence and awe shall touch the life-giving bread beneath the veil that covereth the holy gifts.

Deacon

Let us give heed.

Priest

The holy presanctified things unto the holy.

Here the Priest layeth aside the aer *and continueth with the Divine Office of the Communion.*

[*If it be the Feast-Day of a Saint, or of the church, and the Epistle and Gospel were read, a further short anthem follows here.*]

Choir

One only is holy,[2] One only is the Lord,[3] Jesus Christ, to the glory of God the Father.[4] Amen

O taste and see that the Lord is good.[5]
Alleluia. Alleluia. Alleluia.

---

[1] Deut. 9: 26.   [2] Rev. 15: 4.   [3] Eph. 4: 5.   [4] Phil. 2: 11.   [5] Ps. 34: 8.

In the sanctuary the Deacon standing near the Priest saith

| **Break, O Master, the holy bread.**

And the Priest breaking it in four parts with all heedfulness and awe shall say

| **Broken and divided is the Lamb of God; Which being broken yet is not divided; Being ever eaten, never is consumed; But sanctifieth them that partake thereof.**

And shall let fall the particle into the cup, saying naught. And the Deacon shall pour the warm water into the cup, naught saying, and shall go to stand somewhat apart. And the Priest shall say

| Deacon, draw near.

And the Deacon shall approach and make a devout reverence, entreating forgiveness and saying

| **Lo, I draw near unto our immortal King and God. Impart unto me, O Master, the precious and holy body and blood of our Lord and God and Saviour Jesus Christ.**

And the Priest shall take a single particle from the holy things and give it to the Deacon, saying

| **Unto N., deacon in Holy Orders, is imparted the**

Choir

precious and holy and all pure body and blood of our Lord and God and Saviour Jesus Christ, for the remission of his sins[1] and unto life everlasting.

And the Deacon having kissed the Priest's hand shall withdraw and stand behind the sacred altar, and bowing his head he shall pray, as doth the Priest, saying

| I believe, O Lord . . . [*and the rest, as below*]

And the Priest also taking in the same manner a portion of the holy mysteries saith

The precious and most holy body and blood of our Lord and God and Saviour Jesus Christ is imparted unto me, N., priest, for the remission of my sins[1] and unto life everlasting.

And bowing his head he shall pray, saying

I believe, O Lord, and confess that thou art in truth the Christ, the Son of the living God,[2] come into the world to save sinners; of whom I am chief.[3] And I believe that this is indeed thine incorruptible

Choir

---

[1] Matt. 26: 28.   [2] Matt. 16: 16.   [3] 1 Tim. 1: 15.

body, and this thy most precious blood. Wherefore I pray thee, have mercy upon me, and forgive me my trespasses, voluntary and involuntary, whether of word or deed, witting or unwitting; And vouchsafe that I may partake without condemnation of thy most pure mysteries, for the remission of sins[1] and unto life everlasting. Amen.

Of thy mystical supper, O Son of God, accept me this day as a partaker; For I will not speak of the mystery to thine enemies, nor will I give thee a kiss like Judas;[2] but like the thief I will acknowledge thee: Remember me, O Lord, in thy Kingdom.[3]

And let not this participation in thy holy mysteries be to my judgment nor to my condemnation,[4] O Lord, but unto the healing of soul and body.

And thus they partake of the holy mysteries in fear and with all precaution. Then the Priest shall take the spunge and spunge his hands, saying thrice

| Glory be to thee, O God.

Choir

---

[1] Matt. 26: 28.   [2] Matt. 26: 49; Mark 14: 45.   [3] Luke 23: 42.   [4] 1 Cor. 11: 34.

And having kissed the spunge he shall return it to its place. Then he shall take the chalice with the veil in both hands and drink of it, saying nothing. And wiping his lips and the chalice with the veil in his hands he shall set it on the altar.

And after he hath eaten his pros-phoron *he shall perform the customary ablutions and thereafter still standing somewhat apart shall pray the*

Prayer of Thanksgiving

We give thee thanks,[1] O God and Saviour of all men, for all the good that thou hast bestowed on us, and for the communion of the holy body and blood of thy Christ. And we beseech thee, gracious Lord and lover of mankind, protect and hide us under the shadow of thy wings;[2] And grant us even unto our last breath to partake worthily of thy holy gifts, unto the enlightning of our souls and bodies, and unto the inheritance of the kingdom of heaven.

The Deacon doth not drink from the chalice at this time but after the prayer said by the Priest below the chancel steps, and after the remaining particles

Choir

---

[1] Rev. 11: 17.   [2] Ps. 17: 8.

of the holy mysteries have been consumed. (But if the Priest celebrate alone, without a deacon, he also doth not drink from the chalice after his communion but after the Liturgy is finished and after the holy mysteries have been consumed. For if the wine be sanctified by the placing in it of the particles, yet hath it not been transmade into the divine blood, seeing that the words of consecration are not recited over it in this service as they are in the Liturgies of Basil the Great and John Chrysostom.)

And the Deacon taking the sacred paten and approaching it to the sacred chalice putteth in the holy things, saying naught, and having made three reverences he openeth the Holy Doors.

And the Deacon bowing himself low and devoutly taking up the chalice shall approach the Doors and there lifting up the chalice shew it to the people, saying

In fear of God and with faith draw near.

They that are desirous to communicate shall now approach. They shall come one by one, bearing themselves with all godly humility and awe, with their hands crossed on their breasts. And in this manner each shall receive the divine mysteries.

Choir

I will bless the Lord at all times: his praise shall continually be in my mouth.[1]

---

[1] Ps. 34: 1.

The Priest as he gives communion to each one shall say

The servant of God *** partaketh of the precious and holy body and blood of our Lord and God and Saviour Jesus Christ, for the remission of his/her sins and unto life everlasting.

As each partakes the Deacon shall wipe their lips with the veil, and the communicant shall kiss the holy chalice, incline his head and go aside.

And when all are houselled the Priest goeth into the sanctuary and setteth down the holy things upon the sacred altar.

The Priest shall then turn toward the Holy Doors and bless the people saying

O God, save thy people, and bless thine inheritance.[1]

And the Priest covereth the holy chalice with the veil, and in like manner setteth the asterisk *and the veils over the holy paten.*

And turned toward the sacred altar he censeth it thrice, saying within himself

Be thou exalted, O God, above the heavens; let thy glory be above all the earth.[2]

Choir

Taste ye the heavenly bread and the cup of life; and see how gracious is the Lord.

Alleluia. Alleluia. Alleluia.

---

[1] Ps. 28: 9.   [2] Ps. 57: vv. 5, 11.

And taking the holy paten he setteth it upon the Deacon's head; and the Deacon bearing it with veneration and looking toward the Holy Doors, nothing saying, proceedeth to the offertory-table where he shall set it down.

The Priest in the mean while making a reverence and taking up the holy chalice shall say within himself

| **Blessed is our God;**

And turning to face the Holy Doors and looking to the people shall exclaim aloud

Always, now, and for ever: world without end.

And he beareth the holy things to the offertory-table.

And the Deacon going out by the north door and standing in the accustomed place shall say

Be upright. Having partaken of the divine, holy, undefiled,

Choir

Amen

Let our mouth be filled with thy praise,[1] O Lord, that we may sing of thy glory: for that thou hast accounted us worthy to partake of thy holy, divine, immortal and life-giving mysteries. Preserve us[2] in thy holiness that we may think on[3] thy righteousness all the day[1] long.

Alleluia. Alleluia. Alleluia.

---

[1] Ps. 71: 8.   [2] Ps. 40: 11.   [3] Phil. 4: 8.

immortal, heavenly, life-giving and fearful mysteries of Christ, let us give rightful thanks unto the Lord,

Choir

Kyrie eleison

Succour, save, comfort and preserve us, O God, by thy grace,

Having prayed that this whole eventide be perfect, holy, peaceful and without sin, let us commend ourselves, and one another, and our whole life to Christ our God,

To thee, O Lord

And the Priest folds up the antiminsion and holding forth the Book of the Holy Gospels makes a cross over it saying

For thou art our sanctification,[1] and unto thee we ascribe glory, unto the Father, and unto the Son, and unto the Holy Ghost; now, and for ever: world without end.

Amen

Priest

Let us depart in peace,

In the name of the Lord

Deacon

Let us pray unto the Lord,

Kyrie eleison

Priest standing below the chancel steps

O Almighty Lord who didst create all things in wisdom, and by thine ineffable providence and great goodness hast brought us to these solemn fast-days, for

---

[1] I Cor. I: 30.

the purification of our souls and bodies, for denial of the passions, for the hope of resurrection; Thou who in the forty days didst deliver unto thy servant Moses the tables of stone engraven by God:[1] O thou who art bountiful enable us likewise to fight the good fight, to finish the course, to preserve undivided the faith.[2] Give unto us power to tread on serpents,[3] to be victorious over sin, to worship the holy resurrection without condemnation. For blessed and glorified is thy sublime and wondrous name, of the Father, and of the Son, and of the Holy Spirit; now, and for ever: world without end.

Choir

Amen

Blessed be the name of the Lord from this time forth and for evermore[4]   [*thrice*]

Reader

Glory be to the Father, and to the Son, and to the Holy Ghost; now, and for ever: world without end. Amen.

The Reader now recites **Psalm 34**

I will bless the Lord at all times: his praise shall continually be in my mouth.

---

[1] Deut. 9: vv. 9–10.   [2] 1 Tim. 6: 12; 2 Tim. 4: 7.   [3] Luke 10: 19.   [4] Ps. 113: 2.

Reader

My soul shall make her boast in the Lord: the humble shall hear thereof, and be glad.

O magnify the Lord with me, and let us exalt his name together.

I sought the Lord, and he heard me, and delivered me from all my fears.

They looked unto him, and were lightened: and their faces were not ashamed.

This poor man cried, and the Lord heard him, and saved him out of all his troubles.

The angel of the Lord encampeth round about them that fear him, and delivereth them.

O taste and see that the Lord is good: blessed is the man that trusteth in him.

O fear the Lord, ye his saints: for there is no want to them that fear him.

The young lions do lack, and suffer hunger: but they that seek the Lord shall not want any good thing.

Come, ye children, hearken unto me: I will teach you the fear of the Lord.

What man is he that desireth life, and loveth many days, that he may see good?

Keep thy tongue from evil, and thy lips from speaking guile.

Reader

Depart from evil, and do good; seek peace, and pursue it.

The eyes of the Lord are upon the righteous, and his ears are open unto their cry.

The face of the Lord is against them that do evil, to cut off the remembrance of them from the earth.

The righteous cry, and the Lord heareth, and delivereth them out of all their troubles.

The Lord is nigh unto them that are of a broken heart; and saveth such as be of a contrite spirit.

Many are the afflictions of the righteous; but the Lord delivereth him out of them all.

He keepeth all his bones: not one of them is broken.

Evil shall slay the wicked: and they that hate the righteous shall be desolate.

The Lord redeemeth the soul of his servants: and none of them that trust in him shall be desolate.

During the prayer below the chancel steps the Deacon shall stand on the right side before the ikon of our Lord Christ, holding his orarion *in his hand and bowing his head until the conclusion of the prayer. And when this hath been said the Priest shall enter through the*

Holy Doors and going to the offertory-table he shall say secretly this prayer the while the remainder of the holy things are being consumed

O Lord our God who hast brought us to these solemn fast-days, and hast made us partakers of thy dread mysteries: Join us to thy reasonable[1] flock, and make us heirs of thy kingdom; now, and for ever: world without end. Amen.

The Priest now cometh forth to stand in his accustomed place and distribute the antidoron.

Priest

The blessing of the Lord be upon you, by his divine grace and loving-kindness, always, now, and for ever: world without end.

Glory be unto thee, O Christ our God and our hope, glory be unto thee.

And a Dismissal is made

May Christ our true God, by the prayers of his most holy Mother; by the power of the precious and

Choir

Amen

Glory be unto the Father, and unto the Son, and unto the Holy Ghost; now, and for ever: world without end. Amen

Kyrie eleison [*thrice*]

Master, give the blessing

---

[1] Rom. 12: 1.

life-giving cross; by the protection of the heavenly bodiless
hosts; through the supplications
of the glorious prophet and forerunner, John the Baptist; of the
holy and all glorious apostles;
of our sacred fathers among the
saints, the great hierarchs; of the
holy, glorious and triumphant
martyrs; of our sacred fathers
whom God inspired; of the holy
and righteous progenitors of God,
Joachim and Anna; of N. [*the saint
to whom the church is dedicated*]; of
N. to whose memory we dedicate
this day; of our father among the
saints, Gregory Dialogos; and of
all the saints, have mercy upon
us, and save our souls: For he is
good and loving-kind.

Choir

Amen

(*The Priest pronounceth the foregoing
benediction at the end of the Divine
Liturgy of the Presanctified during the
first weeks of the Lenten Fast. But
Holy Week has a different Dismissal.*)

*The Priest goeth into the sanctuary and
saith the Prayers of Thanksgiving.*[1]
*After which he shall recite the Song of
Simeon,*[2] *the* Trisagion *and the rest,
and the Lord's Prayer. And thereupon
the*

Dismissal troparion

O blessed and glorious
Gregory, endowed with divine

---

[1] See page 211.   [2] *Nunc Dimittis*, Luke 2: vv. 29–32.

grace from God on high, and
strengthened by his might,
thou didst choose to walk in
the way of the Gospel. Wherefore hast thou received in
Christ the reward of thy
labours. Do thou intreat him
to save our souls.

Glory be to the Father, and
to the Son, and to the Holy
Ghost;

And the kontakion

O Gregory our father, thou
hast shewn thyself a shepherd
like unto Christ the shepherd,[1]
leading companies[2] of monks
to the heavenly fold, and from
there hast taught to his sheep
the commandments of Christ:
And now thou dost rejoice with
exceeding great joy[3] with them
in the height of heaven.[4]

Now, and for ever: world
without end. Amen.

And the Hymn to the Mother of God
And the conclusion as shewn on page 101

Choir

HERE ENDETH THE OFFICE OF THE
DIVINE LITURGY OF THE PRESANCTIFIED GIFTS

[1] John 10: 11; Heb. 13: 20.   [2] Acts 6: 7.   [3] Matt. 2: 10.   [4] Job 22: 12.

PRAYERS OF THANKSGIVING
TO BE USED AFTER PARTAKING OF THE
HOLY COMMUNION

When thou hast partaken of the life-giving and mystical gifts praise God straightway. Give much thanks and say with a fervent soul

Glory be to thee, O God.   Glory be to thee, O God.   Glory be to thee, O God.

And then these prayers of thanksgiving

I thank thee, O LORD my GOD, for that thou hast not rejected me, a sinner, but hast suffered me to be a partaker of thy holy things. I thank thee that unworthy as I am thou hast enabled me[1] to receive of thy most pure and heavenly gifts. And yet more over I beseech thee, O Lord and lover of mankind, who for our sakes didst die and rise again, and hast provided[2] us these dread and life-giving mysteries unto the benefit and hallowing of our souls and bodies: Grant that these thy gifts may be even unto me for the healing of soul and body, and the driving out of every adversary; for the enlightning of the eyes of my understanding,[3] and peace for the powers of my soul; for faith unashamed, and love without dissimulation;[4] for the fulness of wisdom, and the keeping of thy commandments; for the increase of thy divine grace, and an inheritance in thy kingdom.[5] That preserved by them in thy holiness I may be ever mindful of thy grace, and not henceforth live unto myself but unto thee,[6] our bountiful Lord.

And when I have departed this life in the hope of life everlasting, vouchsafe that I may enter into eternal rest, where the voice of them that flourish[7] is unceasing, and the delight of them that behold the unsearchable beauty of thy countenance knoweth no bound: For thou art the true desire and the ineffable joy of them that love thee, O Christ our God, and all creation doth sing thy praise, for ever and ever. Amen.

---

[1] 1 Tim. 1: 12.   [2] Gen. 22: 8.   [3] Eph. 1: 18.   [4] Rom. 12: 9.   [5] Eph. 5: 5.
[6] 2 Cor. 5: 15.   [7] Ps. 72: 7.

2. *A Prayer of S. Basil the Great*

LORD CHRIST our GOD, King of the ages and Maker of all things: I thank thee for the blessings that thou hast bestowed on me, and for the communion of thy pure and life-giving mysteries. Wherefore I beseech thee, gracious Lord and lover of mankind, protect and hide me under the shadow of thy wings;[1] And grant me even unto my last breath to partake of thy sacred gifts, worthily and with a clean conscience, for the remission of sins[2] and unto life everlasting.[3] For thou art the bread of life,[4] the well-spring of holiness, the giver of all good; And unto thee we ascribe glory, together with the Father and the Holy Ghost; now, and for ever: world without end. Amen.

3. *A Prayer of S. Simeon Metaphrastes*

O THOU who didst gladly give me thy flesh for nourishment;[5]
Who art fire to consume the unworthy:
Burn me not, O my Creator,
But search out my members. Quicken my reins and my heart.[6]
Let thy flame devour the thorns of all my transgressions.
Purify my soul. Sanctify my thoughts. Knit firm my bones.
Enlighten my senses. Pierce me with thy fear.
Be thou my continual shield.[7] Watch over and preserve me
from every word and deed that corrupt the soul.
Purge me and wash me clean and adorn me.
Order my ways, give me understanding and enlighten me.
Make me the temple of thy Holy Ghost,[8]
and no more the habitation of sin,
that as from fire all evil, every passion, may flee from me
who through Holy Communion am become a place for thy dwelling.
I bring unto thee all the saints to make intercession:
The ranks of the heavenly host;
Thy Forerunner; the wise apostles;
And withal thy pure and holy Mother.
Their prayers receive, O merciful Christ,
and make thy servant a child of light.
For thou art our hallowing.

---

[1] Ps. 17: 8. [2] Matt. 26: 28. [3] John 6: 47. [4] John 6: 35. [5] Col. 2: 19. [6] Ps. 26: 2.
[7] Gen. 15: 1. [8] 1 Cor. 6: 19.

Thou only art the brightness of our souls, O gracious Lord:
and we rightly give glory to thee, our Lord and our God,
all the days of our life.

4. *Another Prayer*

LORD JESUS CHRIST our GOD, may thy sacred body be for me unto life everlasting, and thy precious blood unto remission of sins.[1] May this Eucharist be for me unto joy, health and gladness. And at thy dread second coming, account me, a sinner, worthy to stand on the right hand of thy glory: By the prayers of thy most holy Mother, and of all the saints.

5. *Another Prayer*
To the most holy Mother of God

Most holy MOTHER of GOD, who art the light of my darkened soul; my hope, my refuge and shelter; my comfort and my joy: I give thee thanks for that thou hast suffered me, unworthy as I am, to be a partaker of the pure body and precious blood of thy Son. Do thou who didst bring forth the true light, enlighten the eyes of my understanding.[2] Thou that gavest birth to the fountain of immortality, quicken me who am slain by sin. Thou who art all compassion, O Mother of the merciful God, have mercy upon me, and bestow on me the spirit of remorse and a contrite heart. Give me lowliness of mind.[3] Loose my captive thoughts. And vouchsafe that even unto my last breath I may without condemnation receive the hallowing of the most pure sacrament unto the healing of soul and body. And grant me the grace of repentance and confession that I may praise and glorify thee all the days of my life. For blessed art thou and all glorious for ever and ever. Amen.

And thereupon the Song of Simeon[4]

Lord, now lettest thou thy servant depart in peace, according to thy word:
> For mine eyes have seen thy salvation,
> Which thou hast prepared before the face of all people;
> A light to lighten the Gentiles, and the glory of thy people Israel.

---

[1] Matt. 26: 28.   [2] Eph. 1: 18.   [3] Phil. 2: 3.   [4] *Nunc Dimittis*, Luke 2: vv. 29–32.

The Trisagion

O holy God, Holy and Strong, Holy and Immortal, have mercy upon us. [*thrice*]

Glory be to the Father, and to the Son, and to the Holy Ghost; now, and for ever: world without end. Amen.

Most Holy Trinity, have mercy upon us. O Lord, purge away our sins.[1] O Master, pardon our transgressions. O holy One, visit and heal our infirmities, for thy name's sake.[1]

Lord, have mercy. [*thrice*]

Glory be to the Father, and to the Son, and to the Holy Ghost; now, and for ever: world without end. Amen.

The Lord's Prayer

Our Father which art in heaven, Hallowed be thy Name, Thy kingdom come, Thy will be done, in earth as it is in heaven. Give us this day our daily bread; And forgive us our trespasses, As we forgive them that trespass against us; And lead us not into temptation, But deliver us from evil.

Priest

For thine is the kingdom, the power and the glory, of the Father, and of the Son, and of the Holy Ghost; now, and for ever: world without end. Amen.

Then after the Liturgy of S. John Chrysostom
Troparion *to S. John Chrysostom*

Grace shone forth from thy lips like a flame of fire to illumine the universe. Thou didst teach us to neglect the treasures of this world. Thou hast shewn unto us the height of divine humility. Thou whose words are for our admonition,[2] O Father John Chrysostom, pray unto Christ the Word that our souls be saved.

Glory be to the Father, and to the Son, and to the Holy Ghost;

---

[1] Ps. 79: 9.   [2] 1 Cor. 10: 11.

And the kontakion

From on high didst thou receive grace divine, and the words of thy lips instruct all men to worship one God in the Holy Trinity. O blessed Saint John Chrysostom, we rightly praise thee, for thou art our guide who dost manifest things divine.

After the Liturgy of S. Basil the Great

Troparion *to S. Basil the Great*

Thy voice is gone out into all the earth,
O father among the saints,
Basil the Great, archbishop
of Caesarea in Cappadocia.
All peoples have received thy word,
wherewith thou didst teach fitly of God;
wherewith thou didst expound
the nature of all things;
and didst adorn the manners of men.

O holy father, royal priesthood,
pray to Christ our God
that our souls be saved.

Glory be to the Father, and to the Son, and to the Holy Ghost;

And the kontakion

Rock-like foundation of the Church
hast thou shewn thyself,
dispensing unto all men dominion inviolate,
sealed by thy testimony,
O Basil proven by heaven most holy.

After the Divine Office of the Presanctified Gifts

Troparion *to S. Gregory Dialogos*

O blessed and glorious Gregory, endowed with divine grace from God on high, and strengthened by his might, thou didst choose to walk in the way of the Gospel. Wherefore hast thou received in Christ the reward of thy labours. Do thou intreat him to save our souls.

Glory be to the Father, and to the Son, and to the Holy Ghost;

And the kontakion

O Gregory our father, thou hast shewn thyself a shepherd like unto Christ the shepherd,[1] leading companies[2] of monks to the heavenly fold, and from there hast taught to his sheep the commandments of Christ: And now thou dost rejoice with exceeding great joy[3] with them in the height of heaven.[4]

Now, and for ever: world without end. Amen.

And the Hymn to the Mother of God

O steadfast help and shield[5] of Christians;
Constant advocate with the Creator:
Despise not the prayer[6] of sinners who intreat thee;
But of thy goodness be swift to succour us
that call upon thee in faith.
Make speed to pray. Make haste to intercede for us,
O Mother of God who dost ever watch over them that honour thee.

Lord, have mercy. [*12 times*]

More honourable than the cherubim,
and past compare more glorious than the seraphim,
Who inviolate didst bear God the Word,
Very Mother of God, thee we magnify.

---

[1] John 10: 11; Heb. 13: 20.   [2] Acts 6: 7.   [3] Matt. 2: 10.   [4] Job. 22: 12.   [5] Ps. 115: 9.
[6] Ps. 102: 17.

Glory be to the Father, and to the Son, and to the Holy Ghost; now, and for ever: world without end. Amen.

Lord, have mercy. [*thrice*]

Master, give the blessing.

Priest

May Christ our true God, [*if it be a Sunday* who is risen from the dead,] by the prayers of his most holy Mother; of our sacred fathers whom God inspired; and of all the saints, have mercy upon us, and save our souls: For he is good and loving-kind.

AMEN

INTROIT

UPON SEVERAL OCCASIONS

At the Little Entrance there shall be sung on
The Exaltation of the Precious and Life-giving Cross

Exalt ye the Lord our God, and worship at his footstool; for he is holy.[1]

The Nativity of Our Lord, or The Birth-day of Christ, commonly called Christmas Day

I have begotten thee from the womb before the morning. The Lord sware, and will not repent, Thou art a priest for ever, after the order of Melchisedec.[2]

The Epiphany

Blessed is he that cometh in the name of the Lord: we have blessed you out of the house of the Lord. God is the Lord,[3] and hath revealed himself[4] to us.

The Presentation of Our Lord in the Temple

The Lord hath made known his salvation: his righteousness hath he revealed in the sight of the heathen.[5]

The Transfiguration of Our Lord

O Lord send out thy light and thy truth: let them lead me; let them bring me unto thy holy hill.[6]

The Sunday next before Easter, Palm Sunday

Blessed is he that cometh in the name of the Lord: we have blessed you out of the house of the Lord. God is the Lord,[3] and hath revealed himself[4] to us.

---

[1] Ps. 99: 5.   [2] Ps. 109: vv. 3–4 (*Septuagint*); Ps. 110: vv. 3–4.   [3] Ps. 118: vv. 26–7; Matt. 21: 9; Mark 11: 9; Luke 13: 35.   [4] 1 Sam. 3: 21.   [5] Ps. 98: 2 (marginal reading).   [6] Ps. 43: 3.

Easter Day and the Week following

Bless ye God in the congregations, even the Lord, from the fountain of Israel.[1]

The Ascension of Our Lord Jesus Christ

God is gone up with a shout, the Lord with the sound of a trumpet.[2]

Whitsunday

Be thou exalted, Lord, in thine own strength: so will we sing and praise thy power.[3]

In the place of the Trisagion *there shall be sung on*
The Third Sunday in Lent
and at
The Exaltation of the Precious and Life-giving Cross (September 14)

Thy cross, O Master, do we worship, and thy holy resurrection we glorify.

And on
Christmas Day
The Feast of the Epiphany
The Eve of Palm Sunday
Easter Eve
Easter Day and the Week following
Whitsunday

As many of you as have been baptized into Christ have put on Christ.[4] **Alleluia.**

---

[1] Ps. 68: 26.   [2] Ps. 47: 5.   [3] Ps. 21: 13.   [4] Gal. 3: 27.

THE
DISMISSALS

pronounced Upon certain Feasts and Holy-Days at the Conclusion of Vespers, Matins and the Liturgy, in compliance with the rubric.

The Nativity of Our Lord, or The Birth-day of Christ, commonly called Christmas Day

May he who for our salvation was born in a stable, and laid in a manger,[1] Christ our true God, by the prayers of his most holy Mother; [*and so forth*]

The Circumcision of Our Lord Jesus Christ

May he who for our salvation when eight days were accomplished for the circumcising did think it proper to be obedient to the law,[2] Christ our true God, by the prayers of his most holy Mother; [*and so forth*]

The Epiphany

May he who for our salvation was baptized of John in Jordan,[3] Christ our true God, by the prayers of his most holy Mother; [*and so forth*]

The Presentation of Our Lord in the Temple

May he who for our salvation deigned to be held in the arms of Simeon, a man just and devout,[4] Christ our true God, by the prayers of his most holy Mother; [*and so forth*]

The Transfiguration of Our Lord

May he who in the high mountain of Tabor was transfigured in glory[5] before his holy disciples and apostles, Christ our true God, by the prayers of his most holy Mother; [*and so forth*]

---

[1] Luke 2: vv. 7, 12.   [2] Luke 2: vv. 21–3.   [3] Matt. 3: 13.   [4] Luke 2: vv. 28, 25.
[5] Matt. 17: vv. 1–2.

The Sunday next before Easter, Palm Sunday

May he who for our salvation deigned to sit on a young ass,[1] Christ our true God, by the prayers of his most holy Mother;   [and so forth]

The Same Sunday at Vespers

May he who was content to suffer death in the flesh[2] for our sakes, Christ our true God, by the prayers of his most holy Mother;   [and so forth]

Thursday in Holy Week

May he who of his bountiful goodness didst shew unto us the most excellent path of humility when he washed the disciples' feet[3] and did condescend[4] to us even unto the cross and burial, Christ our true God, by the prayers of his most holy Mother;   [and so forth]

Matins of Good Friday

May he who for the salvation of the world was content to be spat upon and scourged;[5] Who suffered the soldiers to smite him with their hands;[6] Who was crucified and buried, Christ our true God, by the prayers of his most holy Mother;   [and so forth]

Good Friday at Vespers

May he who for us men and for our salvation was content to suffer cruel chastisement and death upon the life-giving cross, and of his own voluntary will[7] was buried in the flesh, Christ our true God, by the prayers of his most holy Mother;   [and so forth]

Easter Day and the Week following

May Christ our true God who is risen from the dead, who death by death hath overcome, and to them in the grave hath given life, by the prayers of his most holy Mother;   [and so forth]

---

[1] John 12: 14.   [2] 1 Pet. 4: 1.   [3] John 13: 5.   [4] Rom. 12: 16.   [5] Matt. 27: vv. 30, 26; Mark 15: vv. 19, 15; John 19: 1.   [6] John 19: 3.   [7] Lev. 1: 3.

The Ascension of Our Lord Jesus Christ

May he who in glory ascended from us into heaven and now sitteth on the right hand of God the Father, Christ our true God, by the prayers of his most holy Mother; *[and so forth]*

Whitsunday

May he who sent down the Holy Ghost upon the disciples and apostles, appearing unto them cloven tongues like as of fire[1] from heaven, Christ our true God, by the prayers of his most holy Mother; *[and so forth]*

The Same Sunday at Vespers

May he who emptied himself from the divine bosom of the Father, who came down from heaven upon the earth and took upon him our whole nature, and divinified it; and thereafter ascended into heaven and sitteth on the right hand of God the Father; Who furthermore did send down upon his holy disciples and apostles the divine and Holy Spirit, which is of one substance with himself, equal[2] in power and glory, co-eternal, thereby enlightning them and through them the whole world: May Christ our true God, by the prayers of his most holy Mother; *[and so forth]*

---

[1] Acts 2: 3.   [2] John 5: 18.

GLOSSARY

Aer A square silken veil (q.v.) covering both chalice and paten.

Anaphora The Great Eucharistic Prayer extending from *The grace of our Lord* . . . (pp. 71 and 119) to the end of the Intercession (pp. 80 and 135).

Antidoron The remains of the *prosphora* (q.v.) offered in the setting forth of the holy gifts, after the Lamb and other particles have been excised at the offertory-table. Cut up and distributed at the close of the Liturgy.

Antiminsion A consecrated corporal of white silk (on which is printed a picture of the Entombment of Christ) with relics sewn into the upper border. Formerly used when no consecrated altar was available for the Liturgy. Now laid on the altar.

Artos Bread brought as offering for bloodless sacrifice (Eucharist) with wine, in form of *prosphora* (q.v.).

Asterisk Two curved metal shafts with a star at the centre. Placed on the paten to prevent the veil from touching the elements.

Catechumen Literally, a hearer. One under instruction.

Cherubicon Hymn sung at the Offertory before and after the Great Entrance. (See pp. 59 and 62–3; 107 and 111.)

Enarxis ('Beginning') The Office consisting of three antiphons and three prayers, with accompanying litanies, which forms an introduction to the Liturgy.

Epigonation Square piece of material hung from the *zone* (q.v.) and resting on the right thigh. Formerly worn only by bishops; now accorded to certain priests as a mark of distinction.

Epitrakhelion The stole of bishops and presbyters. Generally a broad strip (with an opening at the end through which the head is passed) hanging in front and confined by the *zone* (q.v.).

Kontakion Short hymn expressing the content of a feast or praise to a saint.

Orarion Deacon's stole. A narrow strip worn hanging back and front over the left shoulder of the *stikharion* (q.v.), except at the Communion, when it is wound crosswise about the body.

Phelonion The chasuble of the Priest.

Piscina The basin in which the ministers wash their hands.

Prokhimenon   Verses usually, though not always, from the Psalms. (On Wednesdays from the *Magnificat* Luke 1: vv. 46–55.) Sung antiphonally before the Scripture reading.

Prosphoron   ('Oblation') A round leavened loaf about 5 × 2 in., stamped on the top with a 2 in. sq. divided by a cross into four squares in which are severally inscribed IC XC NI KA—that is, 'Jesus Christ conquers'. At the *prothesis* (q.v.) this square is cut out from the loaf and is called the *Holy Lamb* or *Holy Bread*; and at the Fraction it is divided along the lines of the cross.

Prothesis   Offertory-table whereon the elements are placed in readiness for use in the Eucharistic Office.
The term *prothesis* also indicates the preparation of the elements (cf. p. 23).

SAINTS

Antony the Great	*c.* 250–355. Father of Egyptian monasticism.
Antony of Pechersk	First of the hermits to settle in the caves (*peshchery*) outside Kiev. *c.* 1051.
Athanasius	Archbishop of Alexandria from 328 to 373.
Athanasius of Athos	*c.* 960. Founder of the coenobitic monastic life on Mt. Athos.
Barbara	3rd century. Beheaded by her pagan Greek father.
Basil the Great	*c.* 330–79. Archbishop of Caesarea in Cappadocia, 370–9.
Cosmas and Damian	Brothers, physicians, martyred in Cilicia, *c.* 297.
Cyril	Patriarch of Alexandria, 412–44.
Cyrus and John	Alexandrine physicians, martyred *c.* 305.
Demetrius	Patron of Thessalonica where he was martyred *c.* 306.
Ekaterina of Alexandria	Martyred in the 4th c.
Euphemia	Martyred in the 4th c.
Euthymius	377–473. Founder of a monastery between Jerusalem and Jericho.
George	A Cappadocian military tribune. Martyred at Nicomedia, 303.
Gregory the Theologian	Of Nazianzus. Bishop of Sasima in Cappadocia, 370–9. Archbishop of Constantinople, 381.
Gregory Dialogos (the Great)	*c.* 540–604.
Hermolaus	Priest of the Church of Nicomedia. Martyred *c.* 304.

Joachim and Anna	Parents of the Holy Virgin. Not mentioned in the Gospels. Veneration founded on ancient tradition (*Protoevangelium* of James).
John Chrysostom	344/354–407. Archbishop of Constantinople, 398–407.
John Damascene	Born in Damascus in the latter half of the 7th c. Eminent theologian of the whole Christian Church. Spent much of his life in the Monastery of S. Saba.
Kyriaka	Martyred in the 4th c.
Nikolas of Myra	Bishop of Myra in Lycia, early 4th c.
Onuphrius	4th c. Egyptian solitary.
Panteleimon	Physician converted to the faith by S. Hermolaus. Martyred at Nicomedia, *c.* 306.
Paraskeva	Martyred in the 2nd c.
Saba	439–531. A Cappadocian. Founder of the Monastery of S. Saba in the Kidron Valley between Jerusalem and the Dead Sea.
Seraphim of Sarov	1759–1833. Best known of the Russian saints. Thaumaturge.
Sergius of Radonezh	*c.* 1314–1392. Founder of the Troitski Monastery near Moscow.
Simeon Metaphrastes	Compiled a *Lives of the Saints*. Died in the last quarter of the 10th c.
Simeon the New Theologian	949–1022. Priest and *hegumen* (superior) of the Monastery of S. Mamas in Constantinople. Left many writings, both general for all Christians and specialist for those engaged in spiritual warfare.
Thekla	Converted to Christianity at the age of 18 by St. Paul. Lived to the age of 90.
Theodore Stratelates	A soldier of Amasea in Pontus. Martyred at Heraclea in Thrace, 319.
Theodore Tiron	A soldier of Amasea in Pontus. Martyred *c.* 306.
Theodosius of Pechersk	d. 1074. Founder of the Pecherski Monastery at Kiev.
Stikharion	Tunic corresponding to the Western alb but not now of linen, nor always white. The priest's *stikharion* is girded (see *Zone*), the deacon's not so.
Throne	In the dialogue between the Priest and the Deacon on p. 46 'the throne on high' means the Bishop's Throne in the east of the apse and often, especially in old churches, in an elevated position.

Trisagion	The hymn 'O Holy God, Holy and Strong, Holy and Immortal, have mercy upon us'.
Troparion	Any short hymn in rhythmical prose.
Veils	(1) The first veil with which the paten and *asterisk* are covered. (2) The second veil with which the chalice is covered. (3) The *aer* (q.v.) with which both are covered.
Zeon	Warm water added to the chalice before the communion of the clergy and the people.
Zone	Waistband with which the priest's *stikharion* (q.v.) is girded, and his *epitrakhelion* (q.v.) confined.